Caribbean Ants

SELECTED POEMS

Homero Pumarol

Translated from the Spanish by
Anthony Seidman

SPUYTEN DUYVIL
New York City

Translation © 2020 Anthony Seidman

ISBN 978-1-952419-40-9

Cover: from an untitled painting by Carlos Goico

Library of Congress Cataloging-in-Publication Data

Names: Pumarol, Homero, 1971- author. | Seidman, Anthony, translator.
Title: Caribbean ants : selected poems / Homero Pumarol ; translated from
the Spanish by Anthony Seidman.
Description: New York City : Spuyten Duyvil, [2020] |
Identifiers: LCCN 2020037214 | ISBN 9781952419409 (paperback)
Subjects: LCSH: Pumarol, Homero, 1971---Translations into English. | LCGFT:
Poetry.
Classification: LCC PQ7409.2.P86 C3713 2020 | DDC 861/.64--dc23
LC record available at https://lccn.loc.gov/2020037214

Contents

Translator's Introduction

Homero Pumarol (1971, Santo Domingo) is considered one of the Dominican Republic's most important contemporary poets. He is celebrated for injecting contemporary idioms, pop culture, and irreverent humor into his country's letters. His most recent title is *Poesía reunida 2000-2011*, published by *Ediciones De a Poco*, 2011. His work has been included in the leading anthologies of Latin American poetry, as well as numerous journals throughout the Spanish-speaking world. He is also one of the founding members of the spoken word rock group *El Hombrecito* and appears on their LP entitled *Llegó El Hombrecito*. Pumarol was kind enough to collaborate on these translations, and we worked via numerous e-mail messages and phone calls from my apartment in Los Angeles to his in the colonial center of Santo Domingo, the oldest "Western" city in the Americas, and home to the most ancient Cathedral and university; it is a rich stew of Afro-Caribbean rhythms, rum, *merengue* and *perico ripiao*, as well as literary giants, such as Henriquez Ureña, Juan Bosch, Manuel del Cabral, and a history of the Trujillo dictatorship, American occupations. One must not forget the complicated relationship with Haiti, the Republic created from a Slave revolt, and which currently occupies one third of the island of Hispaniola. The energy churning in Pumarol's poetry rises from that complicated list of elements. His experience of living in the United States infuses his verse with an international outlook, and one can discern the influence of such North American poets as William Carlos Williams and Pound in his work. It also comes from his time living abroad in Mexico City, his love of his country's music as well as Bob Dylan's and Lou Reed's, and the unique way in which he incorporated contemporary world poetry into his aesthetics. Just as William Carlos Williams sought an "American idiom", so does Pumarol seek an idiom that echoes what is heard on the streets and plazas of "suelo quisqueyano", the Dominican isle.

CARIBBEAN ANTS

CARIBBEAN ANTS*

One imagines the Caribbean
an ant-swarm devouring the Antilles

and the Antilles as bottles
of different sizes conserving
all of the world's rum

and the world like a baseball
soaring over the roofs of Boston

and Boston is the image that satellites transmit
when Big Papi slowly jogs past second base,
waving to the bleachers, caressing the infield with his cleats

and the cleats are Puma-brand skiffs
carrying 400,000 undocumented travelers
scoffing at the gringo coastguard radars, from *Borinquen*
and back to *Borinquen* by way of Michigan or New York

and everyone has a cousin in the Mona Passage

and one Mona isle is a rooster used for training fighting cockerels
in Bayahibe beach for example there is a cockerel discotheque
where the cockerels dance beneath a disco ball
and tourists dance with spurs while splattering feathers and blood
and the cockerels place bets on the tourists
and the tourists fall in love with the cockerels
and in the end there's a dead cockerel or tourist
and a tourist gets married with the winning cockerel.

Which all has to do with enormous waves of *sanky-pankies***
sliding down the back of a European or Gringo family
and with enormous waves of 1970's engines
rising over highways of beans and rice
among Caribbean ants and bottles of rum.

As with many poems by Homero Pumarol, the title was written originally in English.

**Dominican slang for gigolos*

Caribbean Ants

Uno se imagina el mar Caribe
como un hormiguero que devora las Antillas

Y las Antillas como botellas
de distintos tamaños donde
se conserva todo el ron del mundo

Y el mundo como una pelota
que vuela sobre los techos de Boston

Y Boston es la imagen que muestran los satélites
cuando el Big Daddy trota lentamente por segunda,
saludando a los bleachers, acariciando la media luna con los spikes

Y los spikes del Big Daddy son unas yolas Puma
donde viajan cuatro mil indocumentados
burlando los radares de los guardacostas gringos hasta Borinquen
y de Borinquen a Michigan o a Nueva York

Y todo el mundo tiene un primo en el Canal de la Mona

Y una mona es un gallo manilo que se usa para entrenar gallos de pelea
en Bayahíbe por ejemplo hay una gallera discoteca
donde los gallos pelean bajo un discoball
y los turistas bailan con espuelas salpicando plumas y sangre
y los gallos apuestan a los turistas
y los turistas se enamoran de los gallos
y al final hay un gallo o un turista muerto
y un turista que se casa con el gallo ganador.

Todo lo que tiene que ver con enormes olas de sanki pankis
bajando por la espalda de una familia europea o gringa
y con enormes olas de motores setenta
subiendo carreteras de arroz y habichuelas
entre hormigas Caribe y botellas de ron.

Pangolita*

"Day and night
a little gray police car
follows me"
Luis Días

Every night around three a.m.
a patrol car passes my street,
a Volkswagen Bug,
a rabid and long lasting toy
built in some German oven
dating from World War II.

First, you listen to the motor...
sounds like it's coughing...congested;
next you see the revolving lights
while the little car scurries
along the asphalt like a cockroach.

From here you sniff the odor
of rust, smoke and gasoline
remaining in the air;
the policemen's sweat
smells of menthol and beer,
yet their polyester uniforms and kepis
don't smell like anything.

White and green, the toy
turns the corner, vanishes from sight;
while the reflection of red and blue lights
quickly slides across the city walls
until there's darkness and the street seems real
like a child gazing at me from beneath the table.

*Dominican slang for a patrol car.

PANGOLITA

"A mí me persigue
De noche y de día
Un carrito gris de la policía"
Luis Días

Todos los días después de las tres de la mañana
pasa por mi calle una patrulla de policía
-Volkswagen, "cepillo".
Un juguete rabioso y duradero
fabricado en algún horno de la Alemania
de la Segunda Guerra Mundial.

Uno primero escucha el motor,
parecería que tiene catarro;
luego se ven las luces que giran
mientras el carrito se desliza
sobre el asfalto como una cucaracha.

Desde aquí se siente el olor
a óxido, humo y gasolina
que queda en el aire;
el sudor de los policías
huele a mentol y cerveza
y sus uniformes y quepis de polyester
no huelen a nada.

Blanco y verde el juguete
dobla la esquina y se pierde de vista;
el reflejo de las luces rojas y azules
resbala en los muros un rato
hasta que otra vez oscura la calle parece real
y me mira como un niño debajo de una mesa.

THE FLYING FLEA CIRCUS OF H.P.

When she left me I had
a lawyer and two mechanics left over.
I was so bored that everyday I audited
the plantains and rice.
I became intimate with a washing machine
until my luck ran out and I broke my leg.

When she left me I lost faith in animals,
I started to buy the telephone cat food
and give the mirror ketamine.
For me, the sky was space for smoke,
my life changed so much that I grew out a beard
and my skin turned into a bathrobe.

When she left me I turned in a flea-tamer
and now I wander the streets with a miniature flying circus,
an amazing show that will drain your veins.

THE FLYING FLEA CIRCUS OF H.P.

Cuando ella me dejó yo tenía
un abogado y dos mecánicos atrás.
Estaba tan aburrido que todos los días le hacía
una auditoria a los plátanos y al arroz.
Me hice íntimo de una lavadora
hasta que mi suerte cambió y me rompí una pierna.

Cuando ella me dejó perdí la fe en los animales,
comencé a comprarle comida para gatos al teléfono
y a darle ketamina al espejo.
El cielo para mí era espacio para humo,
mi vida cambió tanto que me creció una barba
y mi piel se convirtió en bata de baño.

Cuando ella me dejó me hice domador de pulgas
y ahora recorro las calles con un circo volador en miniatura,
un espectáculo sorprendente que te secará las venas.

END OF THE CARNIVAL

The military parade has finished.
Only bums stroll the pier,
now an alley where no one finds a peaceful death.

This year there were fireworks
and the President read a tear-jerking
and ovation-worthy speech,
followed by a minute of silence for three
pilots who died while performing supersonic pirouettes.

The military parade has finished.
No more military drumrolls.
No more patriotic canon shots,
or pageantry of horses with polished boots.

Just where did they get so many uniforms?
Will they have to wash and return them
tonight, or tomorrow at dawn?
How will the frogmen and the new SWAT team
while their time away for the rest of the year?

Thirty thousand uniforms
saluted the presidential dais.
And now that litter
leaps and scatters across the streets,
what beds will accommodate such a contingent?

Fin del Carnaval

Ha terminado el desfile militar
y sólo vagabundos pasean por el malecón
que ahora es un callejón donde nadie desearía morir.

Este año hubo fuegos artificiales
y en su discurso el Presidente
supo sacar lágrimas y aplausos
y un minuto de silencio por los tres
pilotos muertos en las piruetas aéreas.

Ha terminado el desfile militar,
se acabaron los redobles,
los cañonazos patrióticos
y la marcha de caballos de botas lustradas.

¿De dónde habrán sacado tantos uniformes?
¿Tendrán que lavarlos y devolverlos
esta misma noche o mañana por la mañana?
¿Qué pasará con los hombres rana
y con el nuevo escuadrón SWAT el resto del año?

Treinta mil uniformados
saludaron la tarima presidencial.
Ahora, cuando sólo se escuchan
papeles arrastrarse por las calles,
¿Qué camas acogerán tal contingente?

SAHARA

At dawn
while I write poems
my bed remembers the Sahara.
I leave to brew coffee,
to see if I also stumble on an idea
like a camel.
Waves of sand whip against my body,
once again I'm awake,
I wrap myself in the sheets
and 5:15 at dawn
my mother and father appear.
They speak very quickly,
like two Bedouin traffickers,
I make out words, I remain silent,
he's on his way to Higüey.
They steal my coffee and, giving me kisses,
my mother puts me to bed.
I open my eyes in *The Thousand and One Nights*,
my mother is a fakir, my father a sultan,
I am a foreign slave,
I try to escape,
I always get lost in the Sahara.

SAHARA

En la madrugada,
mientras escribo poemas,
mi cama recuerda el Sahara.
Salgo a hacer café,
a ver si además tropiezo con una idea
como con un camello.
Olas de arena azotan mi cuerpo,
otra vez estoy despierto,
me envuelvo en las sábanas
y a las cinco y cuarto de la madrugada
aparecen mi madre y mi padre.
Hablan muy rápido,
como dos traficantes beduinos,
entiendo palabras, no hablo,
él va para Higüey.
Roban mi café y dándome besos
mi madre me acuesta.
Abro los ojos en *Las mil y una noches*,
mi madre es faquir, mi padre sultán,
yo soy un esclavo extranjero,
trato de escapar,
siempre me pierdo en el Sahara.

I Suffer From Poor memory

I always confuse the verses in poems,
and so I prefer to write short ones.
My sister Larissa wrote long poems which
were published in the Sunday Book Section,
and when she was ten years old she appeared on T.V.
during the last episode of Capitán Espacio*, who died of AIDS,
(there still needs to be a poem written for Capitán Espacio).
Now she has a husband and three children,
but she died as a poet a long time ago.
She had her own voice, but little future as a poet.
My uncle Julito died of lung cancer
clutching his notebook wherein he copied verses by Lorca
which he used to get girls into his bed.
He didn't have his own voice, but he knew the value of a poem.
I have such poor memory that if they lend me a car
I end up in the precinct to file a report that it was stolen.
Thus, when family and friends ask about me
everyone agrees that I am a "poet",
that I was born to write and will probably die writing poems,
but don't you ever even think of lending him your keys.

*A popular children's television character in the Dominican Republic during the 1980's.

No Tengo Muy Buena Memoria

Siempre confundo los versos de los poemas,
por eso prefiero escribir poemas cortos.
Mi hermana Larissa escribía poemas largos,
que publicaban los suplementos culturales sabatinos
y cuando tenía diez años apareció en televisión
en el último programa del Capitán Espacio, que murió de SIDA
(Queda pendiente hacerle un poema al Capitán Espacio).
Ahora tiene esposo y tres hijos,
pero murió como poeta hace ya mucho tiempo.
Tenía voz propia, pero poco futuro para la poesía.
Mi tío Julito murió de cáncer en los pulmones,
aferrado a una vieja libreta donde copiaba versos de Lorca
que usó toda la vida para llevar muchachas a la cama.
No tenía voz propia, pero sabía muy bien lo que vale un poema.
Yo tengo tan mala memoria que si me prestan un carro
termino en el destacamento declarándolo robado.
Así que cuando preguntan por mí en la familia
todos están de acuerdo en que soy "poeta",
que nací y que probablemente muera escribiendo poemas,
pero que por nada del mundo se te ocurra entregarme unas llaves.

BABYLON BARRACKS

In every door there's an eye,
every hallway's a guessing game,
a stubborn current
like a bird that plummets,
like a scream.

Above each head
a drop sways,
a razor pendulum.

Darkness bastes
the bedrooms
exhausted from hoarse rocking-chairs
and quick cigarettes.

In each window
a wax face melts into
a rusted can of food
amassing ash.

CUARTEL BABILONIA

En cada puerta hay un ojo
cada pasillo es una conjetura
una corriente obstinada
como un pájaro que cae
como un grito.

Sobre cada cabeza
se mece una gota
como un péndulo afilado.

La oscuridad se cuece
en las habitaciones
trabajada por roncas mecedoras
y cigarros veloces.

En cada ventana
se agota un rostro de cera
sobre una vieja lata de alimento
que atesora ceniza.

YEAR OF THE PIG

Of course I believe in the Chinese horoscope,
if not, I wouldn't have returned to this spot
that I love as much as the bed where they strap you down
to administer your first dosage of chemotherapy.
The faces here are coffins,
the medicine containers are rosaries.
In the hallways filled with doctors
one only hears the word of God.
Come, the wheelchairs are scrubbed clean,
the sheets and walls smell of Creolin,
Bibles wait in every drawer;
perhaps we've enough time to toke the Apocalypse.

EL AÑO DEL PUERCO

Claro que creo en el horóscopo chino
si no, no hubiera vuelto a este lugar
que amo tanto como la cama donde te amarran
y te dan tu primera dosis de quimioterapia.
Aquí las caras son ataúdes,
los frascos de medicina son rosarios.
En los pasillos llenos de médicos
sólo se escucha la palabra de Dios.
Ven, las sillas de ruedas están lavadas,
las sábanas y las paredes huelen a creolina,
hay biblias en todas las gavetas,
tal vez nos dé tiempo de fumarnos el Apocalipsis.

COSTA BRAVA REVISTED

For Eddy Bobea

Your shadow grows thinner, thinner;
the street lamps shut my eyes.

The neighborhood houses are mere façades,
a dull world lacking mystery.

To think that you once played beneath those street lamps.
Isn't it like they're spitting in your face?

Crabs revert along the street.
The clatter of their legs on the pavement
shrinks my sadness.

COSTA BRAVA REVISITED

Para Eddy Bobea

Tu sombra se hace cada vez más delgada,
la luz de los faroles me cierra los ojos.

Las casas del barrio son pura fachada,
un mundo plano, sin misterio.

Pensar que tú jugabas debajo de esos faroles.
¿No es como que te escupan la cara?

Cangrejos retroceden por la calle.
El ruido de sus patas contra el pavimento
hace pequeña mi tristeza.

WORDS

When they read my poems
I feel ice-splinters in my temples,
like when one quickly drinks an Icy-Freeze.
When they read my poems
the words paralyze me,
like when you want something
and say the first things that pop in your mind:
ashtray for lighter,
match for cigarettes,
as if you asked for a coffee or vodka
and they brought you a coffin or lantern.
In the end you accept it for what it is,
you got something after all,
and you're not some schmuck who would refuse it,
and with regards to the poem, ah yeah, the poem,
a group of words that someone repeats
and that no longer means a thing to you.

PALABRAS

Cuando ellos leen mis poemas
siento pedacitos de hielo en la sien,
como cuando uno bebe frio-frio rápido.
Cuando ellos leen mis poemas
las palabras me paralizan,
como cuando quieres algo
y dices lo primero que te viene a la mente:
cenicero al encendedor,
fósforo a los cigarrillos,
como si pidieras un café o un vodka
y te trajeran un ataúd o una linterna.
Al final aceptas lo que sea,
algo obtuviste a cambio
y no eres tan imbécil para rechazarlo,
y sobre el poema, ah sí, el poema,
un grupo de palabras que alguien repite
y que ya no significan nada para ti.

THEY ARE GOING TO KILL YOU

Doesn't matter on which side of the bar you find yourself,
the same jig happens each night.
The smoke that gets in your eyes
is the same inflating words.
What's clouding the light isn't some conspiracy,
it's merely the clouds.

The sea flaps like a fish on a tennis court,
and a trash-bag soars like some forgotten night.
The corner beggar won't sleep till paying off the foreign debt.

You turn on another corner darkened by the gospel
while thinking of that woman from a previous night.
In a hallway, you suck her tits ten years later,
but time's up, they're gonna kill you, they're gonna kill you.

That taste of sweet pizza is two bullets.

They Are Going to Kill You

Cada noche se repite lo mismo
no importa de qué lado de la barra estés.
El humo que se mete en los ojos
es el mismo que infla las palabras.
Lo que nubla la luz no es un designio terrible,
son las nubes.

El mar se agita como un pez en una cancha de tenis
y una funda de basura vuela como una noche olvidada.
El mendigo de la esquina no dormirá hasta pagar la deuda externa.

En otra esquina oscurecida por el evangelio
doblas pensando en una mujer de otra noche.
En un zaguán le mamas las tetas 10 años después,
se te acaba el tiempo, te van a matar, te van a matar.

Ese sabor a pizza dulce son dos balas.

POPULAR MONDAY MOVIE

Results from the Latest Election,
results of The Democracy.

Busted sneakers, chicken-bones sucked clean
by a line of drunken strangers.

And now turn on the television, the news,
and light up one mother-in-law and two soap-operas.

Results from the Latest Election,
results of The Democracy.

Three day weekend, chucked stones and domino games,
stray bullets, rationed rum and gasoline.

National Guards in supermarkets, dusk-to-dawn curfew,
fingers of cashiers in hot water.

Results from the Latest Election,
results of The Democracy.

POPULAR MONDAY MOVIE

Los resultados de Las Últimas Elecciones,
los resultados de La Democracia.

Zapatos gastados, huesos de pollo chupados
por una fila de borrachos desconocidos.

Y ahora prende el televisor, El Noticiero,
fúmate una suegra y dos telenovelas.

Los resultados de Las Últimas Elecciones,
los resultados de La Democracia.

Lunes feriado, piedras voladoras y dominó,
balas perdidas, ron y gasolina racionada.

Militares en los Supermercados, Toque de Queda,
los dedos de las cajeras en agua caliente.

Los resultados de Las Últimas Elecciones,
los resultados de La Democracia.

I Like Living In Las Palmas De Herrera

I like living in Las Palmas de Herrera.

The tractors dig ditches and deafen the folk.
The women wreck the sun.
You can sleep in its cots or police station.

I like living in Las Palmas de Herrera.

Urchins chucking rocks at helicopters.
Men looking for shade.
Clouds full of cream.

I like living in Las Palmas de Herrera.

Everything from the grocery store tastes of chicken's blood.

Me Gusta Vivir en las Palmas de Herrera

Me gusta vivir en Las Palmas de Herrera.

Los tractores hacen hoyos y sordos.
Las mujeres arruinan el sol.
Puedes dormir en sus catres o en el destacamento.

Me gusta vivir en Las Palmas de Herrera.

Niños tirando piedras a helicópteros.
Hombres buscando sombras.
Nubes llenas de nata.

Me gusta vivir en Las Palmas de Herrera.

Todo viene del colmado con sabor a sangre de pollo.

Welcome Bienvenida

Adaptation of a plot by W. Carlos W.

To get the key to this door
he had to humiliate himself in front of a booth and apply for a visa,
sell a car, leave family behind, a job, women and friends,
fly across the Atlantic, the Pacific, a layover in Panama;

he had to waste time, always late,
on buses, the metro, in taxis, hungry, wearing flip flops,
until finally getting the first bit of cash bathed in *salsa verde*;

he had to walk faster and speak slower until he lost his accent
he had to endure the first winter abroad without vices nor a television,
until he could land a job and steady pay to rent a room,
get blankets, t.v. set and a thrift shop's leather jacket;

he had to move from *Amores* to *Dolores*, from *Escandón* to *Condesa*,
from Chinatown to Downtown, facing *Papá Jesú*,
where he never paid the electricity bill, and failed as a tenet and was even
accused of being Argentine;

once again, he had to leave stealthily
in a rented truck at daybreak
with a bunch of junk, biscuits, stove and fridge,
piles of dirty laundry and old books,
a girlfriend, three lumpy mattresses and a heater,
—what am I leaving out?—
with light bulbs pilfered from the old apartment;

he had to pay a security deposit of 700 Pesos,
convince the new landlady that he wasn't Argentine,
beg and plead, weep until the rent was lowered to 3,500 Pesos
with only one month's rent in advance,

and also had to look for a security bolt before it got dark,
remove the old lock, install a new one, and hide the spare keys.

And if you're still not sure that the party's here,
leave the bottles and cigarettes behind, and get lost.

BIENVENIDA WELCOME

Adaptation of a plot of W. Carlos W.

Para conseguir la llave de esta puerta
tuvo que humillarse frente a una ventanilla y pedir visa,
vender un carro, dejar familia, trabajo, mujeres y amigos,
volar sobre el Atlántico, el Pacífico y hacer escala en Panamá,

tuvo que andar perdido mucho tiempo, siempre tarde,
en pesero, en metro, en taxi, con hambre, en chancletas,
hasta conseguir el primer billete bañado en salsa verde,

tuvo que andar más rápido y hablar más lento hasta perder el acento,
tuvo que aguantar el primer invierno de prestado sin vicios ni televisor,
hasta conseguir trabajo y dinero seguro para habitación,
frazadas, televisor y una chamarra de cuero de segunda mano,

tuvo que mudarse de Amores a Dolores, de Escandón a Condesa,
del Barrio Chino al Centro, frente al Papá Jesú,
donde nunca pagó la luz, fracasó como rentista y fue acusado de argentino,

tuvo que salir otra vez sigiloso
en un camión rentado de madrugada,
con corotos, biscuises, estufa y nevera,
fundas de ropa sucia y libros viejos,
una novia, tres colchones gastados y un calentador,
-¿qué se me está olvidando?-
con bombillos robados del viejo apartamento,

tuvo que pagar una fianza de 700 pesos,
convencer a la nueva casera de que no era argentino,
rogar, suplicar, llorar hasta bajar la renta a 3,500 pesos
y a un sólo mes por adelantado,

tuvo además que buscar un cerrajero antes de que oscureciera,
quitar la chapa vieja, poner una nueva y esconder las copias.

Y si todavía no estás segura de que aquí es la fiesta
deja las botellas y los cigarros y vete.

MEXICO CITY: JOYRIDE AND POLICE STATION

Here rest the remains of this city within me, but no obituary.
Its taxis roll over my skull,
its lights burn my sky.

Once, I tried to write it a poem
and I woke in fright, running buck-naked
down the street, pursued by a mob screaming Thief!

This city of cathedrals is my hell.
Its angels trail after me, selling me pork cracklings,
its demons stay up all night with my spare change.

Its newspapers and ugly women torment me,
its cantinas thrash me,
its philosophers of soccer turn my rum sour.

This city of bass drums pries itself into my dreams,
barks with my tongue,
and snatches my shoes and good faith.

Once I tried to write it a poem and I woke up in jail.

Ciudad de México, Corrida y Delegación

Esta ciudad yace en mí sin obituario.
Sus taxis ruedan sobre mi cráneo,
sus luces queman mi cielo.

Una vez traté de hacerle un poema
y desperté corriendo desnudo por la calle,
seguido por una turba que me gritaba ladrón.

Esta ciudad de iglesias es mi infierno.
Sus ángeles me siguen, vendiéndome carnitas,
sus demonios se desvelan con mis monedas.

Me atormentan sus periódicos y sus mujeres feas,
me castigan sus cantinas,
sus filósofos de fútbol me amargan el ron.

Esta ciudad de tambores se mete en mis sueños,
ladra con mi lengua,
acaba con mis zapatos y con mi buena fe.

Una vez traté de hacerle un poema y desperté en la cárcel.

TO MY TOES

These clumsy, erratic toes of mine,
pieces from inflexible sticks that
serve for nothing, can't even light a cig
nor hold a goblet.
It's been in vain that I have tried to teach you
how to correctly answer the phone
or forge a signature.
Now help me lift up all of this fat
made from fried chicken and beer,
and see her rise from the bathtub.

To My Toes

Torpes y erráticos dedos de mis pies,
pedazos de palos inflexibles
que no sirven ni para prender un cigarro
ni para sostener una copa.
Muy en vano he tratado de enseñarles
a contestar correctamente el teléfono
o a falsificar una firma.
Ayúdenme ahora a levantar toda esta grasa
hecha a base de pica pollo y cerveza
para verla salir de la bañera.

MOTHERS' DAY

Wine and beer in the freezer,
whiskey, flowers, and air-conditioned living room.
Son-in-law made rice, side dishes,
Larissa brought cashew apple jam,
Mom cooked fillets.

Since our arrival, no one has stopped shouting,
rug-rats screech beneath tables,
two Dachsunds yip each time the bell rings.
Dad recites a sonnet by Napoleón III and about the *Sol de Vancouver*.

We call the corner store
requesting more beer, more cigarettes,
we call San Francisco de Macorís seven times,
three calls to New York,
and one call to Puerto Rico,
until Mom hid the telephone in the closet.

If you want to, you can come over for Mother's Day,
bring *pastelitos* or apple cake or a liter of whiskey,
and you'll leave with a digital photo of you surrounded by twenty strangers,
some red-wine's stain or cigarette's on clothing,
and a dubious explanation regarding Gettysburg.

Día de las Madres

Vino y cerveza en la nevera,
whisky, flores y aire acondicionado en la sala.
Cuñado hizo arroz con vegetales,
Larissa trajo dulce de cajuil,
Mamá cocinó filete.

Desde que llegamos nadie deja de subir la voz,
niños gritando debajo de las mesas,
dos salchichas ladran cada vez que suena el timbre,
Papá recita un soneto de Napoleón III y del sol de Vancouver.

Llamamos dos veces al colmado
para pedir más cerveza y más cigarrillos,
siete veces a San Francisco de Macorís,
tres veces a Nueva York
y una vez a Puerto Rico,
hasta que Mamá escondió el teléfono en el armario.

Si quieres puedes venir el Día de las Madres,
trae pastelitos o quipes o un litro de whisky,
te llevarás una foto digital con más de veinte desconocidos,
alguna caricia de vino tinto o cigarrillo en la ropa
y una explicación dudosa de la batalla de Gettysburg.

MILES AWAY

A black trumpet soars
through the walls
of some rundown building.

Goes faster, further
than this poor night of concrete,
shattered windows and light-bulbs.

Floor-dust is rejuvenated,
words leap from old books,
and now each object speaks of the sweet
and golden aroma from the unique, marvelous sound.

"What will we do when it ends?"
the nail asks the wall.
"Don't know, don't know," says the hammer.

"What will we do when it ends?"
the bottles clamor, and I have no idea,
filling up the hallways and the stairways.

MILES AWAY

Una trompeta negra vuela
a través de las paredes
de un edificio vacío.

Va más rápido y más lejos
que esta pobre noche de concreto
con todas sus ventanas rotas y bombillos.

El polvo en el suelo es renovado,
letras saltan de los libros viejos
y ahora cada objeto habla del dulce
y dorado olor del maravilloso sonido.

¿Qué haremos cuando pare?,
pregunta el clavo a la pared.
Yo no sé, yo no sé, dice el martillo.

¿Qué haremos cuando pare?,
repiten las botellas, yo no sé,
llenando los pasillos y las escaleras.

CAPRICORN

I was born godforsaken, wherever I roam
I seem to drag disaster behind me.

"Now it was bass 'ackwards," my wife screams at me—,
"Beer's hot, and the *chile*'s, cold".

But we have lovely things,
that need an oil change,
like that car. It's going to be vintage.

What songs.
What shirts.
What flowers have we.

We scattered fertilizer in the garden,
and our hair falls out.

You all think I'm crazy,
or that we, the crazy ones, are a bunch of dumb-fucks.

Hearing something break
is like I was saved.

CAPRICORNIO

Nací sin suerte, donde quiera que voy
parezco llevar conmigo el desastre.

Orita estuvo al revés -me grita mi mujer -
La cerveza está caliente y los chiles fríos.

Pero tenemos cosas lindas
a las que hay que echarle aceite
como ese carro. Va a ser un clásico.

Qué canciones
Qué camisas
Qué flores tenemos.

En el jardín pusimos fertilizante
y se nos cae el pelo.

Ustedes creen que yo estoy loco
o que los locos somos pendejos.

Al oír que algo se rompe
es como que me salvé.

REMINGTON

The shotgun arrived at our house over thirty years ago;
Dad bought it from Uncle Próspero
for five thousand Pesos, from back then.

It came in a military case
with a box of red cartridges
and strip of surgical tape stuck to the butt
where once can still read *Próspero Rodríguez*.

It's a brown and black artifact
mixing iron and wood,
and no one could figure out how to use it,
not even on those two occasions when we were robbed.

The house was sold,
my folks brought it to the new apartment
like a spinster aunt.

It's the soul of the house,
an 870 Remington Wingmaster
12 gauge,
eagerly awaiting visitors.

REMINGTON

La escopeta llegó a casa hace más de 30 años,
papá se la compró a tío Próspero
por cinco mil pesos de aquella época.

Vino en un estuche militar
con una caja de cartuchos rojos
y un esparadrapo pegado a la culata
donde todavía se lee Próspero Rodríguez.

Un artefacto marrón y negro,
mezcla de hierro y madera
que nadie nunca supo usar,
ni siquiera las dos veces que nos robaron.

Cuando la casa fue vendida,
mis papás la trajeron al nuevo apartamento
como a una tía soltera.

Es el alma de la casa,
Remington Wingmaster
calibre 12
modelo 870,
y espera ansiosa a que lleguen las visitas.

LIL' POEM

Lil' Poem,
how the odes
that drag on and on and
nobody remembers, envy you!
However, you
stroll through the market
and you even possess a word-or-two
for the dead hens.
The Spaniard, who's a priest
and lover of bad poetry, knows you.
All the whores know you.
All the little girls recite you.
Lil' Poem,
what's this problem you got with dwarves?
You're no Surrealist,
you go inside a pocket and call it landscape.
You go to a burial to praise life.
How you love flowers and mirrors,
and how you abhor oceans,
Lil' Poem.

POEMITA

Poemita,
¿cómo te envidian las odas
que no encuentran final
y que nadie recuerda?
Sin embargo, tú,
te paseas por el mercado
y hasta tienes una frase
para las gallinas muertas.
Te conoce el cura español
amante de la mala poesía.
Te conocen todas las putas.
Te recitan todas las niñas.
Poemita,
¿cuál es tu problema con los enanos?
Tú no eres surrealista,
vas en un bolsillo y dices paisaje.
Vas a un entierro a elogiar la vida.
Cómo te gustan las flores y los espejos,
Cómo aborreces los océanos,
Poemita.

THE FIRST LADY'S MUSTACHE

Nothing like fucking all Sunday
since dawn
not remembering a thing about Saturday,
hitting the streets and looking for trouble,
but not finding a soul out there:
the sky blue, the traffic signals green,
and the dealer at the corner.

What does it matter that your legs
shake all day-long, just
breathe, breathe, breathe.
Or even better: listen to the tunes
of Juan Luis Guerra
according to the Gospel
of Miami Beach,
breathe.

You stop at the corner store,
and leave with two 40's, matches, and a Marlboro
and let them put it on your tab,
by using the First Lady's Mustache.

BIGOTE DE LA PRIMERA DAMA

Nada como singar todo el domingo
desde la madrugada,
sin el menor recuerdo del sábado,
salir a la calle a buscar vicio
y no encontrarse con nadie:
el cielo azul, los semáforos verdes,
el pusher esperando en la esquina.

Qué importa que te tiemblen
las piernas el resto del día,
respira, respira, respira.
Mejor escucha los metales
de Juan Luis Guerra
según el evangelio de
Miami beach,
respira.

Te paras en un colmado y te llevas
dos jumbos cenizas y una Marlboro
y que lo apunten todo en el cuaderno de los fiaos
con el bigote de la Primera Dama.

DEATH WILL COME AND IT WILL BE YOUR MOM

Just whom is that lady addressing,
her mouth eaten by dentures,
shaking her hooves
approaching with eyes like swords
pretending she wants no one,
killing with silence,
filling each second with despair?
It's death, it's death.
Why is she dressed up like my mom?

DEATH WILL COME AND IT WILL BE YOUR MOM

¿A quién se dirige esa señora
con la boca comida por dientes postizos
agitando sus pezuñas
acercando sus ojos como espadas
jugando a no querer a nadie
matando con silencios
llenando cada segundo de desesperación?
Es la muerte, es la muerte.
¿Por qué va vestida como mi mamá?

No Resistance

When they aim a Colt 45 at your head,
four a.m. in the Historic Center,
the first thing you lose is your buzz,
all that money wisely invested
since seven in the evening
usually on beer, as it's the cheapest,
suddenly goes *poof!*
once the icy barrel first
touches your temple.

The cigarettes don't matter much,
but it's bothersome to prove how every mugger smokes,
and he won't even leave you one out of shame.

Then you trudge down the dark street
with the unbearable feeling
that you have just been born
without a Pin Number or Smartphone,
in a world where no one knows you,
and where your rattled nerves matter as much
as the cash you say you once had.

No Resistance

Cuando te ponen una Colt 45 en la cabeza
a las cuatro de la mañana en la Zona Colonial
lo primero que pierdes es la borrachera.
Ese dinero tan bien invertido
desde las siete de la noche
en el menos doloroso de los casos en cerveza,
se esfuma tan pronto el cañón frío
toca por primera vez tu sien.

Los cigarros no importan mucho,
pero molesta comprobar que todo atracador fuma
y que no te dejará ni el de la vergüenza.

Después avanzas por la calle oscura
con la insoportable sensación
de que acabas de nacer
sin BBpin ni Blackberry,
en un mundo donde nadie te conoce
y donde tus nervios importan tan poco
como todo el efectivo que dices que tenías.

THE REPUBLIC

In the central plaza, the Minister of Culture
revealed the names of the poets chosen
to sing new myths about the modern city.
Statues were quickly raised in their honor
and the women cried in ecstasy
when the congress, in order to continue the farce,
declared them to be *poètes maudits*.
So. That's how the feasts commenced, the banquets,
orgies, and the boatload of heavenly sinecures.
All the while I walk away quickly
down hateful avenues and tunnels,
my head uncovered, lacking both hair and laurels,
thinking that I if have no better luck this coming year,
when I return to the city,
it'd be best that I look for another gig.

LA REPÚBLICA

En la plaza pública, el Ministro de Cultura
reveló los nombres de los poetas escogidos
para cantar los nuevos mitos de la ciudad moderna.
Rápidamente se levantaron estatuas en su honor
y las mujeres lloraron extasiadas
cuando el congreso para continuar la farsa
los declaró malditos.
Quedaron así iniciadas las fiestas, los banquetes,
las orgías y demás prebendas de la gloria.
Mientras me alejo a toda prisa
por odiosas avenidas y túneles,
con la cabeza descubierta, sin pelos ni laurel,
pienso que si el año que viene no tengo mejor suerte,
cuando otra vez regrese a la ciudad,
será mejor que busque otro oficio.

THE DEVIL'S DRUM

There are days when the people mob the streets to grab all of it,
they are the terror of the priest who curses them with pus fingers,
they burn the cobweb of old dressers
then make green ashes with new tits.

One dude has tied a drum to his waist
and he plays it wildly and with mad skill.
Another one has pulled out an old trumpet from beneath a cot.
From nowhere, a black man starts to sing,
and he holds hat in hand, waving it solemnly
like Don Juan.

And while the doomed melody dissipates
the afternoon loses its colors
and among the voices of those who got robbed,
someone swears about having seen the devil itself.

The Devil's Drum

Hay días en que el pueblo sale a la calle a ganárselas todas,
son el terror del cura que los maldice con dedos de pus,
queman la telaraña de viejos tocadores
y hacen verdes cenizas con las tetas nuevas.

Uno se ha amarrado un tambor a la cintura
y lo toca impunemente con muchísima maña.
Otro ha sacado una vieja trompeta debajo de un catre.
De ningún lugar un negro ha comenzado a cantar,
lleva un sombrero en la mano que tiende con actitud solemne
como lo haría un tenorio.

Y mientras la malograda melodía se aleja
la tarde pierde sus colores
y entre las voces de la gente atracada
alguien jura haber visto al mismo diablo.

This Is Just to Say

Since 8:30 there's been a power-outage,
mosquitos and heat sweltering all day.
How nice that this morning, before leaving,
you filled the blue bucket.

THIS IS JUST TO SAY

Desde las ocho y media no hubo luz,
el calor y los mosquitos todo el día neceando.
Qué bueno que esta mañana antes de irte,
llenaste la cubeta azul.

THE SUN IS SHINING

For Claudia Rosario

Today the sun came out
and you weren't in my bed.
I had set aside eggs, cheese, bread,
and orange juice for us to enjoy.

I had swept and mopped the floor
so we could walk barefoot
and when once we finished breakfast
we could get back into bed without missing a beat.

It rained all month
and we never saw one another.

But the sun today was red
like the helmet of firefighters,
and its rays illumined the bedroom
as you would when arriving to spend the weekend.

Now that the house is alone
it will start raining at any moment.

THE SUN IS SHINING

For Claudia Rosario

Hoy salió el sol
y tú no estabas en mi cama.
Había guardado huevos, queso, pan
y jugo de naranja para tomarlo juntos.

Había barrido y limpiado el piso
para que pudiéramos andar descalzos
y cuando acabáramos el desayuno
volviéramos a la cama sin perder tiempo.

Todo el mes llovió
y ya nunca nos vimos.

Pero el sol hoy era rojo
como un casco de bomberos
y sus rayos iluminaban la habitación
como tú cuando llegabas de fin de semana.

Ahora que la casa está sola
comenzará a llover en cualquier momento.

THE MADMAN'S INNOCENCE

What can I do with this rain?
Sell umbrellas beneath a traffic light?
Tailor myself a suit made from plastic bags
and go out and push stalled cars for twenty Pesos?

It was conceived for me in a waiting room
among people reading comics from the sport's pages,
it was conceived for me in a cat-house
to cruelly instruct my heart.

Sky gray like a prison roof.
Not a cloud, not a drop, and wind doesn't stir.
The streets have been wet since very early
and the cars, paralyzed by an inexplicable terror.
Heads of old men stretch out from the windows like tortoises,
and I laugh walking along the sidewalk, thinking
how all this happens because of my filthy clothes, my sadness.

THE MADMAN'S INNOCENCE

¿Qué puedo hacer con esta lluvia?
¿Vender paraguas bajo un semáforo?
¿Hacerme un traje a la medida con fundas plásticas
y salir a empujar carros quedados por veinte pesos?

Fue concebida para mí en una sala de espera
entre gente que leía caricaturas deportivas,
fue concebida para mí en una casa de citas
para aleccionar mi corazón con crudeza.

El cielo es gris como el techo de una cárcel.
No se distingue una nube, no cae una gota, no sopla el viento.
Las calles están mojadas desde muy temprano
y los carros están paralizados por un terror inexplicable.
Las cabezas ancianas salen de los carros por las ventanas como tortugas
y yo me río por toda la acera pensando
que todo esto acontece por mi ropa sucia, por mi tristeza.

ONE FOR CARLOS GOICO*

Just last Saturday, we were inside Chapel B,
La Altagracia mortuary,
your smiled rested among electric candles.

We sat, suffocated, remembering
your fauns, your impish devils,
your flowers, and your fishes disguised by paranoid stains,
awaiting a final explanation:
"Look Jaime, look here,
that's a clown rising over the Meriño,
but it's raining and everyone's scattering…"

How heroic it was to listen to Pink Floyd
and leave school.
How horrific to paint inside the insane asylum.

Someone mentioned the mural that made you laugh often,
now buried beneath 50 layers of *Pintura Popular*.
The supernatural heat radiating from that wall of superheroes
painted at night in eggshell, now forever lost.

And a wreath of flowers arrived
from the Academy of Dominican Artists,
something done with such pageantry
that it stretched on our faces the stubborn smile of your last days,
and we went to drink in some less hostile place.

Farewell, Great Dragon of Outer Space,
no longer will there be canvasses to save from the trash,
your cigarette butts will no longer bathe Padre Billini
nor Hostos streets, nor the little Duarte park,
this city will no longer be your ashtray.
What a pity!

*Carlos Goico (Dominican Republic, 1952-2009) was a noted "outsider artist"
who enjoyed popularity during his final years after years of dire poverty
and spending time in mental institutions.

Uno Para Carlos Goico

El otro sábado estuvimos en la capilla B
de la Funeraria La Altagracia,
entre velas eléctricas descansaba tu sonrisa.

Nos sentamos sofocados a recordar
tus faunos, tus diablos cojuelos,
tus flores y tus peces disfrazados de manchas paranoicas,
esperando una última explicación:
"Ve Jaime ve,
eso e un payaso subiendo pol la Meriño,
pero ta lloviendo y tuelmundo corre…"

Qué heroico fue escuchar a Pink Floyd
y abandonar la escuela.
Qué terrible fue pintar en el manicomio.

Alguien mencionó el mural que tanto te hacía reír,
ahora oculto bajo 50 capas de Pintura Popular.
El calor sobrenatural que irradiaba esa pared de superhéroes
pintada de noche con cáscara de huevo, perdida para siempre.

Y llegó una corona de flores
del Colegio de Artistas Dominicanos,
una cosa hecha con tanta necesidad
que nos estrujó en la cara
la obstinada sonrisa de tus últimos días
y nos fuimos a beber a otro lugar menos hostil.

Adiós Gran Dragón del Espacio,
no habrá más lienzos que salvar de la basura,
tus colillas no bañarán la Padre Billini
ni la Hostos ni el parquesito Duarte,
esta ciudad no será más tu cenicero.
¡Qué lástima!

BEHIND THE POLICEWOMAN'S BEHIND

I'm the mugger behind the policewoman's ass,
a blinding reflection I follow down Rafael Augusto Sánchez Ave.,
and I pay no mind to the *mamis* who lead their children to school,
who obey her orders to cross the street,
it's an animal call,
the ass shakes and I drool,
and I follow it beneath a concrete cloud,
down a river of streets and human scraps,
kicking aside dogs and cars,
sniffing fear and cocaine in the alleys,
doing raids and torturing for a cold one.
The policewoman's ass opens my mouth
like the hands of a dentist.

Behind the Policewoman's Behind

Soy el atracador detrás del culo de la policía
es un reflejo ciego que sigo por la Rafael Augusto Sánchez
sin fijarme en las mamis que traen sus hijos al colegio
y que siguen sus órdenes para cruzar la calle
es una respuesta animal
el culo se mueve y yo babeo
y lo sigo bajo una nube de concreto
por un río de calles y chatarra humana
dando patadas a perros y carros
oliendo miedo y coca en los callejones
haciendo redadas y torturando por una fría.
El culo de la policía me abre la boca
como unas manos de dentista.

A Hero for Our Times

Our nightmare gets up wearing our shoes,
swipes the best from dinner, and the worst from the movie theater,
gropes all day while seeking that moment
when we're truly alone.

Today, for example, Wednesday and there's a dry law in effect.
After twelve midnight, the street seethes
like the legs of a boxer on a gurney.

From behind a window a man sells a bottle
of rum as if it were the last dose of heroin,
a old woman waits in line while respecting
that insane habit of obeying which belongs to the poorest:
"Come on, come on, you're the hero of the night,
take the gun from its case and give your woman and son a shot."

Un Héroe de Nuestro Tiempo

Nuestra pesadilla se levanta con nuestros zapatos,
roba lo mejor de la cena y lo peor del cine,
anda a tientas durante todo el día buscando
ese momento en que realmente estamos solos.

Hoy por ejemplo es miércoles y hay ley seca.
Después de las doce de la noche la calle se agita
como las piernas de un boxeador en una camilla.

Detrás de una ventana un hombre vende una botella
de ron como la última dosis de heroína,
una anciana en la fila espera mientras observa
esa insana costumbre de obedecer que tienen los más pobres:
"Vamos, vamos, tú eres el héroe de la noche
saca la pistola del maletín y dale un tiro a tu mujer y a tu hijo."

IN OMEGA WE TRUST

Rain makes it impossible to lower the windows,
stalled cars and destroyed dogs point out the road.
The air conditioning doesn't work,
we sweat and stare at the full pack of cigs.

You speak about needing an iPod
and we end up shouting.
I speak about nature's war waged
on the cardboard houses
and we end up shouting.
You oppose the swindles of a corrupt congress,
any support for the smalltime dealer,
and we end up shouting.

Trucks with no headlights raise waves that we surf
trying to not lose sight of the highway.
Like ants we drink the last drops of hot beer
while thinking that perhaps around the next curve
there will appear a store with cold beer and violent mambo.

In Omega We Trust

La lluvia impide bajar los vidrios,
carros quedados y perros deshechos señalan el camino.
El aire acondicionado no funciona,
sudamos viendo la caja de cigarros intacta.

Hablas de la necesidad de un iPod
y terminamos gritando.
Hablo de la guerra de la naturaleza
contra las casas de cartón
y terminamos gritando.
Opones a la estafa del congreso comesolo
la solidaridad del pequeño narco
y terminamos gritando.

Camiones sin luces levantan olas que surfeamos
tratando de no perder de vista la carretera.
Bebemos como hormigas los restos de una cerveza caliente
pensando que tal vez tras la próxima curva
aparecerá un colmado con cerveza fría y mambo violento.

POSTCARD

Pity you can't see the breakwaters
nor the seagulls or black fishermen along the pier
nor the boats with clouds at the dock as in any postcard
or the café with a view of the sea and ruins of tourists smoking,
drinking, eating Haitian for the first time.
Time here passes according to one's whim,
one or two politicians, a priest and an ambassador.
As the heat's so sweltering,
what needs to get done is done while drunk.
Just like in any province you'll find
a lot of folks ready to recognize
the parish as the national bird, and a lot of women alone,
here, any whore will invite you to a cup of joe.
No matter how much they clean the palm trees,
no matter how large they make the signs,
every year a coconut kills a German.

POSTCARD

Lástima que no puedas ver el rompeolas
ni las gaviotas ni los pescadores negros del malecón
ni los barcos con nubes en el muelle como en cualquier postal
o el café con vista al mar y ruinas de turistas fumando,
bebiendo, comiendo por primera vez haitiano.
Aquí el tiempo pasa como se le antoja
a dos o tres políticos, un cura y un embajador.
Como hace tanto calor,
lo que haya que hacer se hace borracho.
Igual que en cualquier provincia encontrarás
mucha gente dispuesta a reconocer
la parroquia como el ave nacional y muchas mujeres solas,
aquí cualquier puta te invita un café.
Por más que limpien las palmeras,
por más grandes que hagan los letreros,
cada año un coco mata a un alemán.

Nuns

Don't you think that screaming's best,
to grunt like pigs or goats,
squeeze out all our fear at once
until no one can hear us?

Hope weighs heavy,
the silent moments include women,
nuns who eat the day.

They don't know that poetry here
doesn't matter as much as each one of my fingers,
as much as my urge to wring a chicken.

MONJAS

¿Tú no crees que gritar sea lo mejor,
berrear como los puercos y las chivas,
sacarse todo el miedo de una vez
hasta que nadie pueda oírnos?

Las ilusiones pesan,
los silencios figuran mujeres,
monjas que se comen el día.

Ellas no saben que aquí la poesía
no importa tanto como cada uno de mis dedos,
como las ganas que tengo de asesinar un pollo.

This Poem

Once in a while I return to reading this poem.
I like it. Short, and easy to forget.
It has no topic. It goes quickly, no time to spare.
One reaches its end searching for something else.

ESTE POEMA

De vez en cuando vuelvo a leer este poema.
Me gusta, es corto y fácil de olvidar.
No tiene asunto, anda rápido, no tiene tiempo.
Uno llega al final buscando otra cosa.

HEARING VISIONS

For Diego Infante

Visions as real as this house
where the doors are always open
and the lights go out with the moon.

A cat submerges into the trash,
and then leaves it, older
and dragging a fish tail.

Where did that cat come from?
Where the hell did that fish come from?
Is this another real vision or a flashback?
How should I interpret it,
34 years old
and not waiting for any visitors.

OYENDO VISIONES

Para Diego Infante

Visiones tan reales como esta casa
donde las puertas están siempre abiertas
y las luces se apagan con la luna.

Un gato se sumerge en la basura
y sale mucho más viejo,
arrastrando una cola de pescado.

¿De dónde habrá salido el gato?
¿De dónde coño habrá salido el pescado?
¿Se trata de otra visión real o de un flashback?
¿Cómo lo debo interpretar
a mis treinta y cuatro años
y sin esperar visitas?

Garbage from Hell

Learn to play an instrument
and let your beard grow out,
lest Satan recognize you by fate
and you wind up as bones in a sewer.

On Wednesdays, it's two for one at the movies,
and at the city museum
there are women with cars and cheap wine.

Remember this is a land of jealous shotguns,
and that heaven is full of turbaned albinos
and backwash from hell.

Garbage from Hell

Aprende a tocar un instrumento
y déjate crecer la barba,
no sea que por fatalidad te reconozca Satanás
y termines con los huesos en una cloaca.

Los miércoles el cine es dos por uno
y en el museo de la ciudad
hay mujeres con carro y vino barato.

Recuerda que esta es tierra de escopetas celosas
y que el cielo está lleno de albinos con turbantes
y desechos del infierno.

UNDRUNK NO POETRY

On Monday I piss on the bar-top of a saloon
filled with Dominicans
in Patterson, New Jersey,
where William Carlos Williams
probes my liver then shouts at me:
"You better drink faster, undrunk no poetry"
and I've thousands of unpublished poems.

On Tuesday the sheets need to be changed,
Mama Zebu chases me up-and-
down the stairs with a whip in her hand:
"Ya' think this is a hostel, you lil' pisser"
and I've thousands of unpublished poems.

On Wednesday it rains fried eggs and salami
and a voice that was trapped on my worst nights
threatens me with death
and I've thousands of unpublished poems.

On Thursday I'm Haitian,
I trudge barefoot to work,
no one on the street recognizes me
and I've thousands of unpublished poems.

On Friday, I'm a minor celebrity
in the waters of Café De Toi
and I've thousands of unpublished poems.

On Saturday I drink the same
and I've thousands of unpublished poems.

On Sunday, holy hangover
and I've thousands of unpublished poems,
and I've thousands of unpublished poems.

UNDRUNK NO POETRY

El lunes meo en la barra de un bar
lleno de dominicanos
en Patterson, New Jersey,
donde William Carlos Williams
me hace un tacto al hígado y me grita:
"You better drink faster, undrunk no poetry"
y tengo miles de poemas sin publicar.

El martes hay que cambiar las sábanas,
Mamá zebú me persigue
con un látigo por las escaleras
"Tú cree que esto es una pensión meón"
y tengo miles de poemas sin publicar.

El miércoles llueven huevos fritos y salami
y me amenaza de muerte una voz
que se quedó atrapada en mis peores noches
y tengo miles de poemas sin publicar.

El jueves soy haitiano,
voy descalzo al trabajo,
nadie me reconoce en la calle
y tengo miles de poemas sin publicar.

El viernes soy una mini celebridad
en las aguas del Café De Toi
y tengo miles de poemas sin publicar.

El sábado bebo lo mismo
y tengo miles de poemas sin publicar.

El domingo santa resaca
y tengo miles de poemas sin publicar,
y tengo miles de poemas sin publicar.

HELL SEA ROAD

1

The First Lady confers
the Duarte, Sánchez and Mella Medal of Honor
upon a banker
dressed *prêt-à-porter.*

Behind a door
a drunkard is reduced by the law
to something less than trash.

In a cemetery courtyard
beneath a moon equalizing everything
thieves separate teeth from coins.

The sky, black.
The sea, black.
The streets, black.
Black shadows go down the pier
and one confuses demons with fishermen.

Try your luck in this land without tempting the Devil,
and make sure to get drunk with a weapon in your hand.

2

After they fixed the Duarte Highway
one travels from Santiago to Santo Domingo more rapidly,
even if one stops at Bonao to eat magic mushrooms.

After they built the Alcarrizos overpass,
if it doesn't rain, one enters the capital in less time.
But if it rains and one stops to eat magic mushrooms in Bonao,
the Alcarrizos overpass is the antechamber to heaven.

3

It's Friday.
The *mamey* sun is new, the blue sky is new.
Flattened buildings and jalopies
make the landscape more human.

It's Friday.
Black shoes are polished in black puddles.
Motorcycle cops dying from laughter violate women and stoplights.
The street's humidity hastens things
like a thirty year old virgin.

It's Friday.
On this province of an island
the sea's invisible.

HELL SEA ROAD

1

Vestido prêt-à-porter
un banquero es condecorado
por la Primera Dama
con la orden de Duarte, Sánchez y Mella.

Detrás de una puerta
un borracho es reducido por la ley
a algo menos que basura.

En el patio de un cementerio
bajo una luna que lo iguala todo,
ladrones separan dientes y monedas.

El cielo es negro.
El mar es negro.
Las calles son negras.
Sombras negras bajan por el malecón
y se confunden demonios y pescadores.

Corre tu suerte en esta tierra sin tentar al diablo
y procura emborracharte con un arma en la mano.

2

Después que arreglaron la Autopista Duarte
uno llega más rápido de Santiago a Santo Domingo,
incluso si se para a comer hongos en Bonao.

Después que hicieron el elevado de Los Alcarrizos,
si no llueve, uno entra en menos tiempo a la capital.
Pero si llueve y uno se paró a comer hongos en Bonao,
el elevado de Los Alcarrizos es la antesala del cielo.

3

Es viernes.
El sol mamey es nuevo, el cielo azul es nuevo.
Achatados edificios y carros chatarra
hacen el paisaje más humano.

Es viernes.
Zapatos negros se lustran en charcos negros.
Policías motorizados muertos de risa violan mujeres y luces rojas.
La humedad de la calle apresura las cosas
Como una virgen de 30 años.

Es viernes.
En esta isla que es una provincia
el mar es invisible.

TRANSLATOR'S ACKNOWLEDGMENTS

The cover of this collection is taken from an untitled canvas by Carlos Goico, from an exhibition of his work curated by Maurice Sánchez in 2001.

Some of the poems in this book first appeared in slightly different versions in the following journals: *Aji*, *American Journal of Poetry*, *Bitter Oleander*, *Blue Mountain Review*, and *Latin American Literature Today*. Much gratitude.

A special thanks to David Puig and Maurice Sánchez for their assistance, as well as to Amaury Terrero for helping me capture tone and meaning of Dominican idioms and popular culture. An extra dosage of gratitude to the poet for his help during numerous telephone calls and exchanges of e-mails.

HOMERO PUMAROL (Dominican Republic, 1971) obtained the poetry prize named in honor of Pedro Henríquez Ureña in 1997. He is noted for injecting Caribbean Spanish, pop culture, rock n' roll, humor, and the vibrant impasto of the *quisqueyano* experience into the country's poetry. He is the author of four collections, including a volume of new and selected poems entitled *Poesía Reunida: 2000-2011* (Ediciones De a Poco, Santo Domingo). His poems have appeared throughout the Spanish-speaking world in major journals and anthologies, such as *Poesía Dominicana: Antología Esencial* (Colección Visor de Poesía, Madrid). He is also a founding member of the spoken-word rock group El Hombrecito, and he appears on their album *Llegó El Hombrecito*.

Anthony Seidman (1973) is a poet translator born and raised in Los Angeles. His recent translations include *A Stab in the Dark* (LARB Classics) by Facundo Bernal, *For Love of the Dollar: A Portrait of the Artist as an Undocumented Immigrant* (Unnamed Press) by J.M. Servín, and *Smooth-Talking Dog: Selected Poems of Roberto Castillo Udiarte* (Phoneme Media). His newest collection of poetry is entitled *Cosmic Weather*, available from Spuyten Duyvil. He has published translations, poetry and reviews in such journals as New American Writing, The Bitter Oleander, Latin American Literature Today, Poets & Writers, World Literature Today, Poetry International, and Huizache.

Made in the USA
Columbia, SC
28 September 2020

spirit. The third question—Are not these pictures really abstract paintings with literary titles?—gives Rothko the opportunity to frame more explicitly his rejection of the formal modern tradition. Their paintings, he says, are not abstract paintings since it is not their intention either to create or to emphasize a formal color-space arrangement:

> If our titles recall the known myths of antiquity, we have used them again because they are the eternal symbols upon which we must fall back to express basic psychological ideas. They are the symbols of man's primitive fears and motivations, no matter in which land or what time, changing only in detail but never in substance . . .

> Our presentation of these myths however, must be in our own terms which are at once more primitive and more modern than the myths themselves—more primitive because we seek the primeval and atavistic roots of the ideas rather than their graceful classical version; more modern than the myths themselves because we must redescribe their implications through our own experience. Those who think that the world of today is more gentle and graceful than the primeval and predatory passions from which these myths spring, are either not aware of reality or do not wish to see it in art. The myth holds us, therefore, not thru its romantic flavor, not thru the remembrance of the beauty of some by gone age, not thru the possibilities of fantasy, but because it expresses to us something real and existing in ourselves, as it was to those who first stumbled upon the symbols to give them life.

Gottlieb then answers the last question: Are you not denying modern art when you put so much emphasis on subject matter? He states that it is generally felt that the emphasis on the mechanics of picture-making has been carried far enough, and that though the Surrealists had asserted their belief in subject matter, for him and Rothko, "It is not enough to illustrate dreams." Gottlieb continued, stressing the particular situation of artists in 1943:

> If we profess a kinship to the art of primitive men, it is because the feelings they expressed have a particular pertinence today. In times of violence, personal predilections for niceties of color and form seem irrelevant. All primitive expression reveals the

81

constant awareness of powerful forces, the immediate presence of terror and fear, a recognition and acceptance of the brutality of the natural world as well as the eternal insecurity of life.

These views, as romantic as they were, were shared to some degree by other artists of the New York School. A tone of high seriousness had crept into artistic discourse, probably induced as much by a new-found independence as by awareness of the savagery at loose in the world. Rothko and Gottlieb by 1943 were circulating among artists who were feeling excitement in the emancipation of their energies and enjoying a new climate of encouragement. Not the least important in the rapid unfolding of a new vision among American painters was the existence of Peggy Guggenheim's gallery, in which the American aspirants could rub shoulders with stellar Europeans. From 1943 to 1944, the Art of This Century Gallery offered a spate of vanguard American exhibitions, starting with Jackson Pollock's first one-man show in November 1943, introduced by James Johnson Sweeney. He called Pollock's talent lavish, explosive, and untidy, and said that "what we need is more young men who paint from inner impulsion." It was reviewed by Clement Greenberg in *The Nation* enthusiastically, and also by his younger colleague Robert Motherwell in *Partisan Review*, who called Pollock "one of the younger generation's chances." The 1944 season began in October with William Baziotes's first one-man exhibition, followed in late October by Motherwell, and in January 1945, by Rothko.

Rothko's consideration of portraits as ideals that embrace all of human drama was not mere lip service. From around 1943 he had plunged into an atmosphere of perpetual drama and was undergoing the emotional excitement sometimes described in relation to religious conversion. (William James, describing the conversion experience in *The Varieties of Religious Experience*, wrote: "All we know is that there are dead feelings, dead ideas, and cold beliefs, and there are hot and live ones; and when one grows hot and alive within us, everything has to re-crystallize about it.") Rothko's excitement, his unabated attention, his new-found spiritual release, his exhilaration on having, at last, taken the risk Nietzsche had advocated can be felt in the flow of work. He was expanding all his horizons. In the summer of 1943 he had traveled to California, where he first encountered the already notable rebel painter Clyfford Still briefly. In the late fall of 1944 after his separation from his first wife, he met Mary Alice Beistle, whom he married the following March. While he was courting her he gave her a copy of Kafka's *The Trial*. It had appeared in English in 1937 and had ever since been discussed in the little magazines with mounting interest (so much so that by 1947 Edmund Wilson complained that the American literati had produced a cult). Rothko's interest in Kafka was natural enough. He had been a familiar of Kafka's sources in Russian literature, particularly Dostoyevsky; and also of Kierkegaard. As a Jew transplanted into a non-sectarian culture, Rothko was sensitive to Kafka's paradoxes. The entrance to the place of judgment that Joseph K. so fruitlessly sought was, as Rothko said about his own doorways, interpreted as the point at which the artist left the world in which plans and ideas occurred. The parallel world Kafka described, with its deep perspectives giving way to shallow stage sets, and its strange inversions of time and space, was precisely what Rothko was bent on expressing in the works he showed at the Art of This Century. These works represented how he wished to be understood by the world (and how he wished to understand the world, for his views of the nature of art were based on what philosophers had begun to call "intersubjectivity" in the 20th century). They were how he wished to be understood by his fiancée. If he was struck by Kafka's *The Trial*, he was struck by the way Kafka clung to the material world and yet, through distortion, even visual distortion in his strange description of mirrored palaces, endless corridors, simultaneously perceived places of different orders, presented a texture of a world immediately identifiable as mythic; a world in another register, a kind of basso continuo to what Nietzsche called "everyday" life.

The paintings in the first really significant one-man exhibition in Rothko's life, at the age of forty-two, reflected his preoccupations, not only in their suggestive forms, but in their titles as well. On one side there was the Aeschylus atmosphere conjured in the 1942 "Sacrifice of Iphigenia" with its totemic shape, its supplicating hands and robed deity—the transformed Merlin hat. Also "Tiresias," with its emphasis on the seer's eye, and "Hierarchical Birds," its pale

17. *Hierarchical Birds*   c.1944

blues over pinks calling up an Aegean drama; its three divisions offering a frieze effect, and its brushed lines—scallops and chevrons forming a sign language very much like Avery's—evoking the Aeschylean eagle's lament. And again, "The Syrian Bull," "Omens of Gods and Birds," and "Ritual." On the other side there was a group of works reflecting Rothko's preoccupation with a Darwinian vision of the emergence of consciousness, among them "The Birth of the Cephalopods," its thinly layered pinks and golds symbolizing the primordial dawn; and "Slow Swirl by the Edge of the Sea," listed in the catalogue as "Stars and Swirl By at the Edge of the Sea." Recent critics have alluded to Rothko's studies in geology at Yale to account for the layered vision and fossilized forms in "Slow Swirl." They have also suggested that his close relations with Barnett Newman influenced his choice of subject matter. It is possible that in passing, Rothko drew upon his rudimentary knowledge and brief exposure to the natural sciences, and that Newman's keen interest in science, especially ornithology, might have fused with numerous other inflowing interests at this time. It was a time in Rothko's life when the creative afflatus was powerful. All kinds of images and impulses found their way into the paintings that multiplied at an unprecedented rate. In the works exhibited, there were various climates and two main approaches. In "Birth of the Cephalopods" and "Slow Swirl by the Edge of the Sea" Rothko translates his intuition of beginnings through fluidity and the implicit metamorphic character of his arabesques. Here, all is "becoming"—far from scientific causes and effects. In these newly fluent visions, Rothko has almost disembarrassed himself of necessity. The canvas is the one place where such freedom, such an extravagant dream is possible for him. It is the beginning of his exodus from the everyday world, despite his protest that the earthworm was his source. The cephalopods transpire in a spaceless environment peculiar to the dream. In "Slow Swirl"—a painting engraved in the memories of many viewers and justifiably considered a capital summary of the period—the color is etiolated, diffuse: an analogue to an imagined realm where qualities alone, and not the weight of matter, exist. It is the no-color of the sea. The color with no name that so many painters had strived to record, to re-live on canvas, which the sheer matter of oil paint itself has so often defeated. It is as abstract as the *clarté* of which Baudelaire spoke in so many unaccustomed contexts. This triumphal exit from "the world of ideas and facts"; this approach to the "doorway" is the single most significant aspect of the painting. Rothko created his very own light, in the light of which all experience would henceforth be filtered. Within this ambiance there might well be allusions to biologic nuclei, paramecia, surrealist bones, but far more important is the discernible reference to Rothko's secret impulse to rival the art of the musician. There are arabesques, spirals, and clusters of bars that can be read as musical symbols. In the main shapes, the two gyrating figures (that admittedly bear comparison to Ernst, Dalí, Masson, and his own colleague Jackson Pollock) have vestigial feet—an overt reference to the dance. The existence of clef signs and the scrollwork of violins unmistakingly refers to the reception of music, and the clusters of linear flourishes produce movements with distinct rhythmic intentions as their lines intersect. The axis of each figure is vertical, and the figure itself can be understood as a play on the arabesque, an infinity sign.

During the same year Rothko began to work out a slightly different exodus route from the given world of things and events. "Poised Elements" and one or two other works such as "Olympian Play" are characteristic. Here, Rothko defines more precisely the light that could never be associated with the hard objects picked out by the "everyday" light of day. He has discovered the light within the canvas itself, as Miró had before him. He scrapes the surfaces in "Poised Elements" to uncover their inmost threads, and he divides his composition into three zones of experience, inter-related by the rather sharply defined forms. These tiers of reds, grays, greenishgrays shelter certain specific references—to a chrysalis perhaps, and to birds and shadows. Above all, they suggest the mirrored world of interior fantasy; a light of otherness that is the beginning of Rothko's conquest of antinomies. From now on there will be many allusions to white and whiteness as a kind of nimbus, an aura, a natural enough allusion to the ancients who imagined a luminous vapor or cloud hovering about their gods who visited earth.

In this group of works of roughly 1944-46, Rothko is emboldened to use accents of dramatic color, most often red, that bear associa-

86

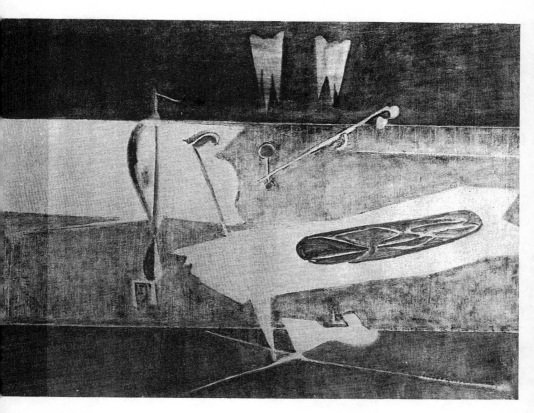

18. *Poised Elements*   1944

19. *Olympian Play*   c.1944

tions with primitive ritual. He also for the first time experimented with saturated blacks, using them to symbolize recession. In this he may have been encouraged by the works of Jackson Pollock exhibited in 1943 at the Art of This Century. Pollock had thrown out the old Impressionist caveat, and was dramatically underscoring his own mythic paintings with liberal areas of harsh blacks. For Pollock, black certainly represented emotional power; for Rothko, darkness and fertility, earth and night.

These paintings in Rothko's first one-man show at Art of This Century in 1945 were introduced with an unsigned foreword (by Peggy Guggenheim's assistant Howard Putzel?) that almost certainly reflected Rothko's own evaluation of his work at the time. Rothko was in the habit of trying to control everything connected with his work, even the written commentary. Elaine de Kooning describes a bizarre encounter a few years later in which Rothko, given an opportunity to read over an article before publication, completely rejected it. When de Kooning offered to re-write it, he insisted on accompanying her to her studio immediately, where he remained all night as de Kooning revised her text. Rothko passed on it page by page between beer and pastrami sandwiches. For a catalogue foreword to what he regarded as his most important exhibition, Rothko would have been no less zealous. "Rothko's style has a latent archaic quality," the writer of the Art of This Century preface asserts. "This particular archaization, the reverse of the primitive, suggests the long savouring of human and traditional experience as incorporated in the myth." We can hear Rothko in the following:

> Rothko's symbols, fragments of myth, are held together by a free, almost automatic calligraphy that gives a peculiar unity to his paintings—a unity in which the individual symbol acquires its meaning, not in isolation, but rather in its melodic adjustment to the other elements in the picture. It is this feeling of internal fusion, of the historical conscious and subconscious capable of expanding far beyond the limits of the picture space that gives Rothko's work its force and essential character. But this is not to say that the images created by Rothko are the thin evocations of the speculative intellect; they are rather the concrete, the tactual expression of the intuitions of an artist to whom the subconscious represents not the farther, but the nearer shore of art.

This statement contains the contradiction that Rothko and others at the time most worried over: the primacy of intuition versus the importance of art as knowledge. Rothko's position was, and would remain, that such antinomies must not be resolved, but must be held in suspension. The writer's last sentence, abjuring the "speculative intellect," was a reflexive gesture of self-defense that most American artists made in the face of the critics who were hostile on both counts.

Rothko's show, that he had hoped would find, finally, critical acclaim, did not make much of a stir. The daily newspapers, that had so recently afforded him so much gratification, ignored it. In the art journals he was favorably but briefly reviewed. The reviewer in *Art Digest* (Jan. 15, 1945) remarked that "Mark Rothko has been a kind of myth in contemporary art for about ten years" and spoke of "the extent of courage a painter must have to make a sortie of this kind into unexplained territory." Rothko, knowing that the state of reviewing at the time required that he explain his unexplained territory, composed a personal statement for an exhibition a month later at David Porter's Gallery in Washington, in which Pollock, Baziotes, and Gottlieb were among the exhibitors. Rothko opened with his familiar insistence that he adhered to the material reality of the world and the substance of things. "I merely enlarge the extent of this reality, extending it to coequal attributes with experiences in our more familiar environment":

> I insist upon the equal existence of the world engendered in the mind and the world engendered by God outside of it. If I have faltered in the use of familiar objects, it is because I refuse to mutilate their appearance for the sake of an action which they are too old to serve; or for which, perhaps, they had never been intended.

Rothko goes on to make a careful distinction that shows he had recourse to philosophical currents then being discussed in New York, currents that would soon become obvious in the Existentialist vocabulary adopted even by the art critics:

> I quarrel with surrealist and abstract art only as one quarrels with his father and mother; recognizing the inevitability and

function of my roots, but insistent upon my dissension; I, being both they, and an integral completely independent of them.

Rothko separates himself from Surrealism, as he had in 1943 statements, on the basis of humanism—the humanism that acknowledged, or rather, fed upon the culture of the ancients in the tragedies. The Surrealists, he said, had established a congruity between the phantasmagoria of the unconscious and the objects of everyday life. "This congruity constitutes the exhilarated tragic experience which for me is the only source book for art." But, he added:

> I love both the object and the dream far too much to have them effervesced into the insubstantiality of memory and hallucination. The abstract artist has given material existence to many unseen worlds and tempi. But I repudiate his denial of the anecdote just as I repudiate the denial of the material existence of the whole of reality. For art to me is an anecdote of the spirit, and the only means of making concrete the purpose of its varied quickness and stillness.

He ends on a resounding note:

> Rather be prodigal than niggardly I would sooner confer anthropomorphic attributes upon a stone, than dehumanize the slightest possibility of consciousness.[26]

This statement was not to be superseded by later statements or even by the seeming abandonment of subject and symbol in his own abstract works. Even after he left behind apparent anecdote, it remained harbored in his imagination. A few years later he was telling students to avoid French-style abstraction and abstracting from the model: "I'd rather paint eyes on a rock, put a couple of eyes on a rock," he told them, "than take the human figure and make it mechanical the way Picasso does. Or Léger."[27]

6

During the 1940s Rothko's life was punctuated with events that sustained his excitement and incited his daring. His intensifying awareness of himself as an individual "I, being both they [roots], and an integral completely independent of them" became evident to friends who noted Rothko's increasing recourse to polemic. Both privately and publicly he harrowed away in the subsoil of his psyche. His need to formulate a philosophy of art was shared by many of his painting colleagues who, after the Second World War, burst into a new round of excited discussion that was to lead to a vague grouping later dubbed Abstract Expressionism. Rothko, always known for his probing conversation and his ability to wield various theories in the Socratic manner (many of his old friends agreed that he could have been a lawyer or a clergyman), redoubled his effort to clarify his own stance. Having already found the Surrealist position wanting, he was open to many alternatives. One of them was presented by the North Dakota-born painter Clyfford Still, whom he had first met in San Francisco in 1943. Still, who was forging a colorful myth about himself even in those days, exercised a powerful attraction for Rothko, the pensive descendant of bookish people. Still was the very personification of the New World pioneer: self-reliant, defiant, pitting himself against nature. He shared the new continent's suspicion of European culture, and was, at least in the myth he proposed for himself, firmly opposed to any intellectualization of art. He talked all the time about "energy and intuition" and about the need to get out from under decadent European influence. He was also given to boasting about his virile youth, in Alberta, Canada, where "my arms have been bloody to the elbows shucking wheat" and where he would take a horse at night for five miles "to bang out Brahms and look at art magazines."[28] Still's fierce independence and his hatred of anything that smacked of "collectivism" impressed Rothko. Still became Archilochus to Rothko's Homer. With his brash rhetoric (interlarded with terms drawn from baseball rather than aesthetics) he both amused and fascinated Rothko. Even early on Still was given to vivid tirades at which he would excel in later years. Motherwell has called him the John Brown of the art world. Rothko, who had never forsaken his anarchist rebelliousness, took Still seriously. When Still arrived in New York in the late summer of 1945, Rothko visited him in his studio in Greenwich Village without being invited (according to Still in his later account thoroughly tinctured with malice). There Rothko saw some of the easel-sized paintings done the year before in Virginia, many of them dark, roughly painted images in which wrench-like or totemic shapes were dramatically lighted in a kind of Götterdämmerung atmosphere. Although Still's sensibility was entirely different from Rothko's, Rothko responded to the drama these canvases undeniably embodied. He reported back to Peggy Guggenheim enthusiastically and persuaded her to visit Still's studio shortly after. She decided to exhibit Still in her autumn opening group show. Soon after, she offered him a one-man show for the following February. In the interim Rothko and Still drew together, although Rothko's other close associates, Gottlieb and Newman, had some reservations about this arrogant newcomer. Rothko seemed to admire Still's arrogance, and Still, despite his later disparagement, decidedly encouraged Rothko's devotion. When the time came for the Art of This Century show, it was Rothko who wrote the catalogue, and we can hardly credit Still's later version that he had not wished Rothko to do it, and that Rothko had used him for his own purposes. Still probably encouraged Rothko's interpretation that tended to identify him with the Art of This Century group (Baziotes, Pollock, Motherwell, Rothko especially), whom Rothko called the "small band of Myth

20. Untitled   1945

Makers who have emerged here during the war." Rothko saw Still expressing the "tragic-religious drama which is generic to all Myths at all times, no matter where they occur" and, with generous intention, declared that Still was creating "new counterparts to replace the old mythological hybrids who have lost their pertinence in the intervening centuries." Finally, Rothko alluded to the Persephone myth and quotes Still himself as saying that his paintings are "of the Earth, the Damned and of the Recreated." Years later, what Rothko remembered writing about Still was about the primal matter from which these paintings were wrung—the environment of the earthworm.

Rothko's encounter with Still's paintings was as fruitful as his encounters with works of other contemporaries from whom he learned. He, who had struggled so mightily to master his means, was heartened to observe, as he had already to some degree discovered in the works of the Surrealists, that a nice technique, such as the French painters seemed to command, was not at all necessary to expression. Still couldn't care less about conventional techniques. He trowelled on his paint with indifference to modulations, concerned only with keeping alive his intuition and displaying his energy. His melodramatic propensity for sharp light effects was evidence that, like Rothko, he thought of painting as a counterpart to theater.

When, in April, Rothko had an exhibition of his watercolors and gouaches arranged by Betty Parsons at the Mortimer Brandt Gallery, the incursion of Still's earthy, damned, and re-created vision in Rothko's imagination was beginning to be visible, but it wasn't until his exhibition of oils at the San Francisco Museum of Art the following August that a distinct note of Still's turbid surfaces is felt in a few paintings, such as "Untitled," in which Rothko uses far more restless shapes than is usually his wont, and where Still's monkey-wrench stylizations as well as his zig-zagging eruptions of light in darkness appear. However, there are familial likenesses in these paintings to Pollock and Motherwell just as much as to Still.

Even Still was susceptible to the gathering group consciousness in the painters' quarters in those days. Painters met on neutral ground, such as the Waldorf Cafeteria, or, in the later 1940s in a few favored taverns, such as Minetta Tavern on MacDougal Street, and later the Cedar Tavern on University Place, and thrashed out their views of what they perceived to be a new situation. Rothko, who did not live downtown and was considered by some artists to be something of a loner, all the same made frequent sorties to find his confreres in the downtown bars. He maintained friendly relations with a number of artists and visited studios regularly. One of the artists who caught his attention during that highlighted season when he had his first important one-man show was the young Motherwell, fresh from serious studies in literature and art history, and eager to test his burgeoning theories with older artists. Rothko liked to talk to Motherwell, and, as in the case of Still, Motherwell probably represented a refreshing change. "I was Stephen Dedalus to his Bloom," Motherwell says. "We were exotic to each other." They had met during the afternoon when Rothko was hanging his show. That spring they saw each other from time to time, and during the summer of 1946, when Rothko had rented a small cottage in East Hampton, they saw each other frequently, dining together at least once a week and having extended conversations. When they returned to New York, Rothko introduced his young friend to his circle, among them Barnett Newman, Herbert Ferber, Adolph Gottlieb, and Bradley Walker Tomlin.

In 1944 Motherwell had given a talk at Mount Holyoke College, "The Modern Painter's World," in which he had addressed himself to questions that were regarded by New York painters as extremely significant. This was published in *Dyn*, a review published in Mexico City and widely read by New York artists. In his article, shaped within the framework of Marxist analysis that he had learned in his studies with Meyer Schapiro during the late 1930s, Motherwell takes cognizance of historical oppositions between painters and the bourgeoisie, but suggests that the experience of the artists who had known Spain, Hitlerian genocide, and the carnage of the Second World War had mitigated the old arguments. The problem for the emergent artist *"is with what to identify himself."* Since in Motherwell's view the middle class was decaying and the working class had forfeited its consciousness, there seemed little alternative for painters but to paint for each other. He too, like Rothko, Newman, Still, Baziotes, and Gottlieb among others, had outgrown the dogmas of Surrealism and specifically rejected their disdain for "the mind" or formal values in painting. He had concluded that painting is "mind realizing itself in color and space. The greatest adventures, especially in the brutal and *policed* period, take place in the mind."

Rothko's mind was working furiously in the latter half of the 1940s. The flow of his work was unabated, and his reflection on its sources gained in depth as he, like so many others at the time, engaged in spirited discussion. The evidence abounds in periodicals and letters of the late 1940s that artists had crept out of their proverbial isolation in American society and were establishing themselves in the intellectual community as valid cultural figures, much to the bemused surprise of a number of literary figures who could never quite believe that this caste of handworkers had much to contribute. There were, however, several members in the artists' milieu who were determined to raise the status of the visual artists via the literary magazines. Harold Rosenberg, who had a foot in both camps, was busy with Motherwell, plotting a new, intellectual artists' publication, while Ruth and John Stephan were readying their quarterly, *The Tiger's Eye*. Both journals appeared in the fall of 1947. *Possibilities*, the Rosenberg-Motherwell project, was destined to have only one issue, but it was an issue brimming with questions and inquiries, brilliantly summing up the preoccupations of the immediate postwar art world. Its most salient attitude was one of disaffection with ideology and politics. These prewar concerns of artists were considered by almost everyone to have been fruitless and naïve. Writers, as Isaac Rosenfeld had noted as early as 1944, who were searching for a "belief broader and more reliable than politics regard this as their only alternative: to go forward by going back into themselves. And even if this is not the only means for making themselves 'men of substance' still they will have found a different means. . . ."[29] Rosenberg, moving in the same circles as Rosenfeld, would be the agent through which this attitude became validated for visual artists. Together with Motherwell, he gave a precise profile to a growing conviction that swept past ideologies and aesthetics, into the unknown. The confluence of streams of thought during the last few years of the 1940s is remarkable. Among the forceful voices emergent then was that of Rothko. In these few years—from 1945 to 1950—artists as varied as Rothko, Gorky, Newman, de Kooning, Pollock, Still were engaged in vigorous debate with themselves and were willing to express their views publicly. They were not young hotheads. They had been schooled during the Depression years, and most were more than thirty-five years of age.

Rothko was forty-four in 1947 and living an intensely exciting moment. His first real success after the Art of This Century show had occurred in the summer of 1946 when the San Francisco Museum of Art held a large one-man exhibition of his work. He visited the West Coast and wrote back to his new dealer, Betty Parsons, that he had found real "adulation." Emboldened by his cordial reception, Rothko had thrown himself into his work with heightened enthusiasm and had redoubled his efforts to define, for himself first, and then for artistic friends, his proper aesthetic terrain. It was an unusually vivid moment in American art history. Rothko's participation in public forums can be seen in the context provided so richly by the two postwar publishing ventures, *Possibilities* and *The Tiger's Eye*, in both of which he offered carefully composed statements of his beliefs.

The Tiger's Eye appeared late in 1947. It was designed as a quarterly and for a time Barnett Newman was an associate editor, inviting his friends—many now represented by Betty Parsons—to contribute statements in a section he called The Ides of Art. Among them were Rothko, Baziotes, Hedda Sterne, Gottlieb, and Herbert Ferber. Newman's aesthetic position was, for a few years, parallel with Rothko's and Gottlieb's. His intellectual bent was more pronounced, however, and he was given to working out his ideas (and sometimes theirs) in written form. In 1945 he had written a manuscript in which he elaborated the themes Rothko and Gottlieb had broached in their *New York Times* letter. They are the themes that he was to introduce in 1947 in *The Tiger's Eye*, and from which he and his friends would most remarkably depart pictorially within just a few months. (The quick evolution of the Abstract Expressionists from semi-abstraction to abstraction is documented almost moment by moment in the publications.) Newman wrote in his unpublished 1945 manuscript:

> After more than two thousand years we have finally arrived at the tragic position of the Greek and we have achieved this Greek state of tragedy because we have at last ourselves invented a

new sense of all-pervading fate, a fate that is for the first time for modern man as real and as intimate as the Greeks' fate was to them. . . . Our tragedy is again a tragedy of action in the chaos that is society (it is interesting that this Greek idea is also a Hebraic concept), and no matter how heroic or innocent or moral our individual lives may be, this new fate hangs over us. We are living then through a Greek drama and each of us now stands like Oedipus and can by his acts or lack of action, in innocence kill his father.[30]

Within two years Newman, and everyone else who had brought "action into chaos" in their works, was pressing beyond the classical sources, though he still maintained that "the central issue of painting is the subject matter, what to paint." It was a sober, and, some would say later, rather humorless period. But the seriousness was beyond dispute. Even Arshile Gorky, who was somewhat disengaged from the group fervor, would write to his sister that "art must always remain earnest . . . Art must be serious, no sarcasm, no comedy. One does not laugh at a loved one."[31] Both publications would stress seriousness, earnestness, urgency, and would reflect the Abstract Expressionists' preoccupations as they worked their way through to total abstraction. Amid advertisements for books by Valéry, Kafka, Lorca, Sartre, and Stein, they scattered their thoughts concerning: the function of metamorphosis in art; moral despair and aesthetic nausea (Kierkegaard was in vogue); the meaning of primitive art; the role of mythology; the question of commentary and its relevance to painting, and the meanings brought home by the unprecedented carnage of the Second World War.

Rothko's two favorite literary sources—Shakespeare and Greek tragedy—were amply treated. In the second issue of *The Tiger's Eye*, Ariel's speech with its T. S. Eliot association, is reproduced. This speech not only addresses itself to mortality, as Rothko insisted painters must, but brings in the rich theme of metamorphosis, endemic to the mythic atmosphere he had already engendered in his work:

> Full fathom five thy father lies
>   Of his bones are coral made;
> Those are pearls that were his eyes:
>   Nothing of him that doth fade,

But doth suffer a sea-change
Into something rich and strange . . .

Shakespeare was also to be the source of the painterly passing beyond. When artists and writers hovered near the gateway to abstraction, they could find strange clues in Shakespeare. Rosenberg in *Possibilities* explores Hamlet's ambivalence and places his emphasis on the endlessly hermetic lines: "Seems, madam! nay it is; I know not seems." When Rothko would shortly after speak of bypassing obstacles, and when he would begin to purge his paintings of allegory, he could say, like Hamlet, "I have that within that passeth show." Hamlet's purification rings through Rothko's statement in the October 1949, issue of *The Tiger's Eye*. He sees clarity as the elimination of all obstacles between a painter and his idea, and between the idea and observer. Rosenberg cites Hamlet's speech:

Yea, from the table of my memory
I'll wipe away all trivial fond records,
All saws of books, all forms, all pressures past,
That youth and observation copies there;
And thy commandment all alone shall live
within the book and volume of my brain
Unmixed with baser matter: yes, by heaven!

Rosenberg's comment is almost a program for those whom he would later, with Hamletian thrust, call action painters:

Feeling himself unable to go forward, he must destroy the accumulations in which he has recognized himself and come to put his trust in the possibilities of the unknown.

This is just what Rothko does in his own meditation in *Possibilities* where he implies a leap into the unfamiliar. Calling his paintings "dramas," he says they begin "as an unknown adventure in an unknown space." His shapes, he says, "have no direct association with any particular visible experience, but in them one recognizes the principle and passion of organisms." Already the trivial fond records and forms and pressures of the past—the "ideas and plans that existed in the mind at the start"—are banished as the adventurer leaves the world in which they occur.

The move toward disembarrassment of the past reflects a consciousness of the bankruptcy—a word the painters often used—of past positions, and a dalliance with the notion of aesthetic despair. Motherwell in the issue of *The Tiger's Eye* in which Barnett Newman's interest in the classic notion of the sublime is explored, speaks of "getting rid of what is dead in human experience" and speculates:

> Perhaps painting becomes Sublime when the artist transcends his personal anguish, when he projects in the midst of a shrieking world an expression of living and its end that is silent and ordered . . . (#6, Dec. 15, 1948)

And Gottlieb in an earlier issue speaks of "a desperate attempt to escape from evil,"

> the times are out of joint, our obsessive, subterranean and pictographic images are the expression of the neurosis which is our reality. (#2)

As the painters tried to find their way in the labyrinth of sources newly examined, they often vacillated between a desire to retain a foothold in the intellectual world of Western civilization, and a desire to achieve the directness, the untramelled activity they imagined the primitive artists enjoyed. In the second number of *The Tiger's Eye*, there is a transcription of Kwakiutl shaman songs, as well as an important excerpt from Paul Valéry that supports the idea that an artist can act, rather than think, his creations:

> The idea of *making* is the first and the most human of ideas. To "explain" is always only to describe a manner of *making*: it is merely to remake by thought. The *Why* and the *How* which are simply expressions for what this idea requires, arise in every context, and insist on being satisfied at any price.

Valéry's importance to the "band of Myth Makers" should not be underestimated. They relished his unorthodox, sometimes aphoristic pronouncements, such as "for that which in us creates has no name; we have merely eliminated all men, *minus one*." Rosenberg was to draw extensively on Valéry's perceptions of the creative process as he worked to give definition to the new activities amongst painters. Baziotes in *Possibilities* chooses a text from *Variété* on

"The Silence of Painters." Those who were thrashing out the issues repeatedly reverted to the classical myths, but little by little their endeavor was transformed into a quest for an absolute that the classical world would not support. Thoughts raced ahead but the paintings reproduced in the magazine often alluded to the ancients. In March 1948 there was de Chirico's "Hector and Andromache," Stamos's "Sacrifice of Cronos," Masson's "Bull Head, Twisted Figures," Gottlieb's "Pictograph," Rothko's "Sacrificial Moment," Gorky's "Agony," and even de Kooning, the least mythic in spirit, has a painting called "Orestes." Newman, beginning his polemic for an American art that distinguished itself from the highly civilized European (reflecting the ambivalence toward Europe, springing from the 1930s and becoming something not so remote from the hated nationalism of that epoch) writes in the same issue that the American in comparison to the European is "like a barbarian"

> He does not have the super-fine sensibility toward the object that dominates European feeling. He does not even have the object. This is, then, our opportunity, free of the ancient paraphernalia, to come closer to the sources of tragic emotion. Shall we not, as artists, search out the new objects for its image?

Shortly after, in the symposium on the sublime in art,[32] he is speaking of "man's natural desire in the arts to express his relation to the Absolute" and again appoints himself spokesman for the Americans who reject "concern with beauty and where to find it"

> We are reasserting man's natural desire for the exalted, for a concern with our relationship to absolute emotions. We do not need the obsolete props of an outmoded and antiquated legend. . . . We are freeing ourselves of the impediments of memory, association, nostalgia, legend, myth, or what have you, that have been the devices of Western European painting.

Along with the new tone of rebelliousness, and a sense of security that American painters had never known vis-à-vis their European fathers, there was a concomitant alertness to everything new that appeared in postwar Europe. The big thinkers still seemed to be anchored there, and the publications the artists wrote in and read, were quick to pick up the new currents abroad. *The Tiger's Eye* respected French intellectuals and printed translations of work by Georges Bataille, Genêt, René Char, and the Surrealists' favorite, the Comte de Lautréamont. In addition, they were attentive to the immediate postwar painters, some of whom were exhibited very soon after the war in New York, among them Fautrier, Matthieu, Michaux, Ubac, and Wols.

Rothko's attitudes were subtly changing as can be seen in his last statement made for *The Tiger's Eye*, October 1949. "The progression of a painter's work, as it travels in time from point to point, will be toward clarity: toward the elimination of all obstacles between the painter and the idea, and between the idea and the observer." Examples of such obstacles he gives as memory, history, or geometry, "swamps of generalization from which one might pull out parodies of ideas (which are ghosts) but never an idea in itself." "The idea in itself," was to become his leading idea. It is very much dependent on the original impulse that had suggested to him that music could be in some way a source of his own means. He wound up his statement confidently: "To achieve this clarity is, inevitably, to be understood." Rothko uses this "understood" in the broadest sense, assuming that the observer is moved, he knows not how, and that through the purity (clarity) of the "idea" comes another kind of knowledge, not dependent on explanations. The brevity of this final statement of the 1940s speaks of his growing conviction that words, words, words, as Hamlet declared, could not substitute for a painter's making his paintings. Both he and Clyfford Still had begun to make an issue of the uselessness of words, and the triviality of art criticism. Still wrote letters to Betty Parsons, and to Rothko, decrying the "scribblers" and insisting on their irrelevance in the face of the painters' great decisions to become totally independent. The abstraction "freedom" began to assume new significance as these two painter anarchists were preparing their assault on the organized art world. Their defiance of what they saw as the vulgarity of the art world is hinted at throughout the late 1940s, but becomes more arrogant in the 1950s. In *The Tiger's Eye* (#2, 1947) Rothko had already suggested the extravagant ethical basis on which they would proceed when he stated that "a picture lives by companionship, expanding and quickening in the eyes of the sensitive observer. It dies by the same token. It is therefore a risky and unfeeling act to send it out into the world. How often it must be permanently impaired by the eyes of the vulgar and the cruelty of the impotent who would extend their affliction universally!" Rothko could easily see that American philistinism was not extinguished, despite the new interest in the band of mythmakers. A touch of the old reformer's ambition was left, and this was kindled by Still's hyperbolic personality. When Douglas MacAgy invited Rothko—at Still's suggestion probably—to come to teach a summer semester at the newly reorganized California School of Fine Arts, Rothko offered not only studio instruction but a series of lectures as well.

The atmosphere at the school was bracing for Rothko. The students admired him, treated him as a master. They knew his work from the preceding year's retrospective, and some, such as Richard Diebenkorn, had spent hours studying "Slow Swirl by the Edge of the Sea" that had remained on view in the museum. Clyfford Still, who had a way of inspiring his students with fierce loyalty, passed them along to Rothko. Even those, who, like Diebenkorn, had found Still's extravagant polemics distasteful, were willing to submit to the more meditative approach Rothko offered. Many of the students were young men who had returned to school on the GI Bill. They were only too eager to believe that there could be a totally new expression in painting. Most were quite willing to hear Still denounce the European forebears and exhort them to follow their intuitions. Under MacAgy's inspired leadership, the school was, as he said, a "wide open situation." Anything could, and was meant to happen there. Still hectored his students and insisted on the ethic in which the painter takes full responsibility for what he does, and protects it from the hostile world. Rothko agreed, and was probably stimulated by the atmosphere in the school—a slightly hysterical atmosphere in which students and teachers, as MacAgy put it, knew they were making history. Rothko was considered a "very inspiring teacher," whom MacAgy described as smoking endless cigarettes, "the curling smoke almost a symbol of how he talked: very elusive talk." MacAgy's attention to Rothko's presence can be gauged in an article—the first serious article on Rothko in an art journal—published in *The Magazine of Art* (January 1949). It can be assumed that MacAgy's interest in Rothko's lectures, coupled with his early recognition of Rothko's distinction as a painter of new subject matter, informed his article. From the beginning he establishes Rothko's effort to give broadly philosophic meaning to his enterprise. Mac-Agy starts by stating that if we subscribe to the notion of painting as a symbolic act, then we can understand what Rothko means when he says that a painter commits himself by the nature of the space he uses. This was, undoubtedly, one of the principles Rothko had enunciated in his lectures. The bold departure from the quantified space of the Renaissance, stressed by the Surrealists, was of great importance to him. MacAgy sees Rothko moving in a space characterized by a continuous fading in and out, existing only as a relationship of things. Rothko himself, the author points out, "refers to the relations between objects and their environment as *dramatis personae* of his paintings" and he speaks of "purposeful ambiguity." MacAgy might be quoting Rothko when he states: "Pictures are episodes of transformation which engage the artist's interests in dramatic action." MacAgy understood (as few others did) that the "theatre of Rothko's imagination" displays the basic assumptions from which philosophies are formed. Although the work is visual, presented through sight, the experiences, MacAgy says, transcend the limits imposed by visible particularities.

MacAgy was referring largely to works produced between 1944 and late 1948, some of which had been exhibited in New York in March 1947 at the Betty Parsons Gallery and again in March 1948. The reviewers were not so prescient as MacAgy. Sam Hunter writing in the *New York Times* (March 14, 1948) accurately described Rothko's art as "an art solely of transitions without beginning, middle or end" but, unlike MacAgy, saw it as "an impasse of empty formlessness." The paintings of 1947-48 were, in fact, ambiguous, showing Rothko feeling his way toward an expression that would directly, without the interference of specific shape, suggest the numinous floating world into which he stepped once his obstacles were left behind. He scraped and thinned his colors. Their edges bled. A form with the most tenuous of edges could slide into another, while atmosphere from one moment to the next could be weighted or lightened. A vocabulary of starts and stops, almost like

21. Untitled   1949

musical notation, is contained here, with short strokes sometimes interrupting longer ones, and rounded forms juxtaposed with long, strand-like shapes, or vertical pole-like shapes, none of which seemed very stable, and all of which were subject to minute transformations. After his show in 1945 Rothko worked often on large watercolor paper with an exceedingly toothy grain. By dragging a dry brush on slightly dampened surfaces he had discovered many ways to suggest mirrored forms, and forms that seemed to emanate their own light. Some of these watercolors were composed with three levels, each illumined differently and each furnished with ambiguous signs relating to the others. No doubt these freely explored motifs, and particularly the surprising effects of light, encouraged the radical changes in his works in oil on canvas. These more abstract works were still "anecdotes of the spirit" and the drama that Rothko had said inheres in a Rembrandt portrait could often be read in moody tones that masked lightly sketched undertones. Rothko had almost worked his way through to the point that he had envisioned in 1943 where "the whole of man's experience becomes his model and all of art is the portrait of an idea." When Harold Rosenberg came to summarize the works of the abstract expressionists, referring specifically to Rothko and Newman, he wrote

> In sum, what the new American artist sought was not a richer or more contemporary fiction (like the Surrealists), but the formal sign language of the inner kingdom—equivalents in paint of a flash, no matter how transitory, or what had been known throughout the centuries as spiritual enlightenment.[33]

The "flash," toward which Rothko had instinctively directed himself, was about to occur.

Private enlightenment was not openly avowed, however, not even to himself. Rothko was caught up in the missionary fervor that motivated many painters during the late 1940s. He still attempted to carry out the public education that had once been the function of the cultural committee of the Federation. It was commonly believed among painters that unless the public—and that included the critics—was taught to see what it saw, it would never see it. The painters were not wrong. There were still very few writers con-

22. Untitled   c.1946

cerned with their work, and, apart from Greenberg and Rosenberg, none from the hallowed literary community. The attitude of most of the literati was one of patronizing wonder. They were convinced that painters were somehow not capable of dealing with thoughts and ideas, and that the burgeoning aesthetic was remote from their own preoccupations at that moment. This persistent secret contempt for the handworker has never completely abated in the United States. When one of *Partisan Review*'s former editors, William Barrett, wrote his memoirs he alluded fondly but patronizingly to the Abstract Expressionists, especially Willem de Kooning and Franz Kline.[34] He recalls giving a lecture on Existentialism at the Artists' Club but noted that "ideas, abstract ideas have a way of bouncing off the minds of artists at curious angles." Barrett shrunk from giving a second lecture: "I remember remarking to one of them that perhaps they had enough of ideas and should stick to their art." He doesn't hesitate to add that the New York School history was to be "an indecent traffic with ideas, in the course of which it is really remarkable that some good painting managed to get done."

In the face of such stubborn prejudice, Rothko and other artists were at once enraged and exasperated. The Club itself was an outgrowth of their frustration in the general culture. It grew out of the discussions Rothko, Still, and MacAgy commenced in 1947 about a school for young painters that would be conducted in an entirely unorthodox manner and would focus on the real problems and ideas the postwar period had spawned. In the fall of 1948, Rothko, Gottlieb, Baziotes, Motherwell, and David Hare founded the school, called, at Newman's suggestion, Subjects of the Artist. A lecture program was initiated, open to the public. For Rothko the stress of the school proved too much (probably the stress of internecine wrangling) and in midwinter he wrote to Still that he was on the eve of a nervous breakdown and was withdrawing from the school, which itself folded in the spring. The lectures continued, sponsored by another group of painters from New York University, and eventually the Friday nights came to be consecrated as the informal entity known as The Club. To this often disorderly and always lively gathering came an assortment of New York intellectuals, curious about *la vie Bohème* personified by the hard-drinking, sometimes rowdy artists. Only a few, however, understood that painters were indeed ploughing in the same fields and using the same "ideas" that they were. The most serious inquiry was undertaken by Clement Greenberg in both *The Nation* and *Partisan Review*, where he wrote regularly about the group. He piqued the curiosity of his timid literary confreres when he wrote of the poverty of the painters, their fifth-floor cold water studios, their "neurosis of alienation," and the increasing sense of wild abandon he felt in the work, particularly of Pollock. Greenberg's doughty prose, and Harold Rosenberg's witty exposition of the general moral atmosphere among these newly invigorated artists, did help to attract an ever-widening audience. But Rothko sensed, perhaps correctly, that this audience, while friendly, was still unable to decipher the new language and was indiscriminate in its taste. Little by little he relinquished his public activities. He turned up rarely at The Club, but sometimes appeared in the favored bars to exchange views with fellow painters. Most of his conversations, however, took place in the homes of the artists with whom he showed at the Betty Parsons Gallery, or in the studios of a few of his more intellectually inclined colleagues.

7

By 1950 Rothko had talked himself, thought himself, into his position and then fallen relatively silent. He had struggled with prevailing ideas, often contradictory: on the one hand, the strong tendency among American intellectuals to endorse practical positivism and on the other, his own instinctive drive toward what Rosenberg had called "the flash." Through it all, he had managed to preserve the original insights drawn from Nietzsche. He still saw his art as an effort to express his sense of tragedy. He had also begun to decipher for himself the language, the nature of the expression, that had been born long before the First World War, and that later, in the hands of Malevich, Mondrian, and a few other absolutists, constituted an authentic way of pictorial thought. Henceforth his arguments with himself would be couched in the esoteric, almost inaudible dialect that had finally revealed itself to him. Perhaps he had taken to heart Nicolas Calas's counsel in the December 1948 issue of *The Tigers' Eye* that "One should listen to the stillness of painting with the awe with which one harkens the silence of deserts and glaciers."

Rothko was no more at ease with life than he had ever been. The "everyday" was still a difficult realm. He was more avid than ever to know, fully, the satisfaction of release from necessity and to "hark to the suspiration/the uninterrupted news that grows out of silence."[35] His new preoccupation with silence had its metaphysical dimension, much as he fought shy of it. Every once in a while, though, a secret yearning shone through his spoken statements, as when he had admitted ironically in *Possibilities* that the primitive artist lived in a more "practical" society where "the urgency for transcendent experience was understood, and given official status."[36] Implicit in his statement is an attack on materialism. He speaks of "the finite associations with which our society increasingly enshrouds every aspect of our environment." He laments solitude. Yet, it was silence and solitude which would lead him to the transcendent experience he implied every society must know in order to be healthy. It was a silence that others were beginning to explore. In the same issue of *Possibilities* in which Rothko was speaking, Baziotes was presenting a text by Paul Valéry called "The Silence of Painters," and Paul Goodman was writing on "primary silence" and Nietzsche.

These silences, paradoxically invoked in a time of much noisy discussion, had their origins in Europe and were transmitted in many untraceable ways to American artists. Rothko was susceptible on the deepest level—he had long been familiar with the "uninterrupted news" while at work. Since late 1945 he had managed to live in the vicinity of the Museum of Modern Art and could drop in whenever the spirit moved him. It moved him frequently in the late 1940s and early 1950s. There, in an atmosphere considerably more calm than it is today, he could study the permanent collection, in which certain works had their permanent place. Alfred Barr and René d'Harnoncourt had installed the permanent collection sensitively. The silence of certain modern precursors was reverently respected. As if to stress the point, Redon's painting in the high symbolist manner, in which a thinly painted, ethereal personage holds a silencing finger to its lips, remained for years in the first room of the permanent collection. Its relation to Matisse would not be overlooked.

It was to Matisse that Rothko gravitated with renewed interest. In his old concourse with Milton Avery the polite respect awarded Matisse was apparent. But in his new frame of mind, Rothko could respond to Matisse's radicalism without reserve. Years later he would call upon his wife as witness, recalling how he had spent hours and hours and hours before "The Red Studio" once it was permanently installed in 1949. It was of crucial importance to him he later thought. Having come so far himself in conjuring an atmosphere uniquely other than the "everyday," Rothko could confirm many of his intuitions through the study of "The Red Studio." The paradox implicit in Matisse's firm statement was poignantly alive to Rothko. Matisse presents what can be read as a room, a studio, with a number of identifiable objects—brushes, dishes, jugs, chairs, easels, stools, plants, sculptures, paintings, and a clock. There are things there, things that bespeak a human presence, things that are used in everyday life, things that Rothko admired Avery for being able to incorporate in his life's work. And yet, these "things," with which Rothko himself was so ill at ease, were not really there—as Matisse was careful to emphasize—*as* things. Their barest outlines were merely absences that became outlines, as Matisse left the white of the canvas around them. Their presence was to be a virtual presence in an overwhelming atmosphere that Matisse announced as whole; as, in fact, a personal cosmos. The centered clock gives the circular time and the objects rotate within a whole, irradiated with an inner light that was always Matisse's goal. "The destination," as he said so often, "is always the same." If he worked with thinly layered paint in impeccably modulated reds, it was to achieve the dreamed-of unity that could be found in the light of the mind.

This disembodied light had visited Matisse as a youth and he never renounced it. It was part of the tradition that he claimed and sustained throughout his life—the tradition so brilliantly expounded in the French Symbolist movement. Throughout his painting life Matisse reflected the principles implicit in the Symbolist attitude toward reality. Once he had passed his psychological condition of being a student, he had thought ceaselessly of the meanings inherent in his painting and had found them consistent with the meanings adduced by the Symbolists. Art exists not to represent the world as it is lived day by day, but to create a parallel world—a "condensation of sensations." He would, he said, sacrifice charm in order to seize the essential character of what he is painting. "Underneath this succession of moments which constitutes the superficial existence of beings and things, and which is continually modifying and transforming them, one can search for a truer, more essential character." For him, "all is in the conception." Therefore, he must have a clear vision of the whole from the beginning. All of this Matisse stated by 1908.[37] Toward the end of his life, he was still speaking of his "internal vision": "Thus a work of art is the climax of long work of preparation. The artist takes from his surroundings everything that can nourish his internal vision, either directly, when the object he is drawing is to appear in his composition, or by analogy."[38] This analogy, to which Matisse often refers in his interviews and statements, is the spirit of analogy articulated by the poet Mallarmé, whose poems Matisse read early in the morning "as one breathes a deep breath of fresh air." Mallarmé had told himself as a youth that he must purify language and use it so that it could "describe not the object itself but the effect it produces." He spoke of "a spiritual theater" and an "inner stage" where absences (equivalent to the whites Matisse employed) evoked his inner drama. The objects in his poems were to be assembled in the receiver's imagination symbolically. "Things exist, we don't have to create them, we simply have to see their relationships," Mallarmé wrote, "Our eternal and only problem is to seize relationships and intervals, however few or multiple." On his part, Matisse observed: "I don't paint things, I only paint differences between things."

Matisse had not been insensible to the long tradition going back to Baudelaire and Delacroix in which the "musicality" of painting was perceived as more significant than the individual motifs within a painting. He had studied the works of their natural heirs—Gauguin and Cézanne—assiduously. Gauguin's words, well known to painters emerging in the 20th century, clearly echoed Mallarmé's;

> My simple object, which I take from daily life or from nature, is merely pretext, which helps me by means of a definite arrangement of lines and colors to create symphonies or harmonies. They have no counterparts at all in reality, in the vulgar sense of that word; they do not give direct expression to any idea, their only purpose being to stimulate the imagination—just as music does without the aid of ideas or pictures—simply by that mysterious affinity which exists between certain arrangements of colors and lines in our minds.[39]

It was to this view, epitomized by Mallarmé, that Matisse, and, through Matisse, Rothko, gravitated. Until Rothko undertook his most taxing adventure into the unknown that he had said was the artist's province—the mural series that dominated his last phase—he was playing out the lessons implicit in the symbolist tradition. He had said he wanted to raise painting to the level and poignancy of poetry and music. The Symbolists had begun the project, and he was to extend it beyond their most extravagant dreams.

His means was painting, and only painting, but revery was its source. Releasing the "slow swirl" of revery was as familiar an occupation to him as walking or smoking a pipe, as he had in his youth. He could entertain in his reveries the possibility of miracle,

> Pictures must be miraculous: the instant one is completed the intimacy between the creation and the creator is ended. He is an outsider. The picture must be for him, as for anyone experiencing it later, a revelation, an unexpected and unprecedented resolution of an eternally familiar need.[40]

Like other painters of his generation, he searched the horizons of many ages, including his own, in order to find miraculous expressions of eternally familiar needs. Increasingly the silences of certain epochs and artists inspired his reveries. He must have stood many times before the Pompeian frescoes installed at the Metropolitan Museum, where he frequently went to study Greek and Roman antiquities. The calm figures of Pompeian matrons and the presences of the gods, repose in a hushed place in a perfect harmony of parts. The reds, from pomegranate to crimson, are genially faded, urging upon the viewer still more the remoteness of the dream-ridden characters. The Pompeian way was largely theatrical. There is always the breath of theater in the way the painters provide a shallow stage and an appropriate backdrop. What is occurring here? Not even the owners of the villa knew exactly. Years later, when Rothko finally saw Pompeii itself, he met with familiar emotions. The House of Mysteries, with its grave and hermetic theatrical rites, meets his Nietzschean requirements. Rothko recognized himself in Pompeii. His recognition of himself and his own purposes occurred long before he was recognized, or rather, understood by those outside his inner circle of friends. Unlike Pollock and de Kooning, Rothko, as Motherwell has pointed out, suffered from not

23. Rothko at Betty Parsons Gallery, New York, 1949

having a strong advocate. Each time he exposed himself to the appraisals of others he was met with either hostile incomprehension or reticent, mumbled praise, with only very rare exceptions. He tried to brazen it out. In *Possibilities* he had consoled himself with the thought that in the absence of an embracing approving community the artist gains in freedom. "Both the sense of community and of security depend on the familiar," he had written. "Free of them, transcendental experiences become possible." All the same, he longed for others to recognize in his work the resolution of "an eternally familiar need." That was to remain in abeyance for a long time to come. In the late 1940s and early 1950s, his exhibitions at the Betty Parsons Gallery met mostly with such bewildered responses as Margaret Breuning's (*Art Digest*, April 15, 1949), who remarks that "schoolroom Latin comes to mind in viewing the exhibition of Mark Rothko's paintings at Betty Parsons Gallery, for Virgil's *disjecta membra* exactly sums up the impression of these amorphous works." Thomas Hess in *Art News* was much more sympathetic, although he too limited his remarks as though he were awaiting further enlightenment. He notes Rothko's "wild contrasts of color" and that "under this extremely emotional level is a strength of composition which is almost Oriental." It would be several years before Hess would write with strong conviction about Rothko's paintings. Even then, if the literature on Rothko during the 1950s is surveyed, it will be seen that he attracted far fewer serious articles than many of his colleagues in the New York School, and often even his most admiring commentators could not conceal questions and doubts that were rarely raised in the case of the others. No one with any knowledge of New York School painting would have doubted his importance, or underestimated his radical gesture. But something was withheld; some intangible sign of understanding for which Rothko was longing. The unreserved response, and the more searching approach to his work would come, eventually, from Europe and England.

It is not surprising. Europeans were backed by a tradition to which Rothko's aspirations could easily be assimilated. They quite naturally apprehended the expression in Rothko since they themselves had been working in parallel directions, in which a convergence of previous expressions and theories flowered after the Second World War. Nietzsche had been resurrected in France first by Gide and later to serve the Existentialists. In France poets, philosophers, and painters were undertaking an intense inquiry into the nature of space and how man inhabits it, and the nature of the human drama and how man interprets it. Sartre and Merleau-Ponty were fashioning their fresh theories of perception, in which they often called upon artist witnesses, and Camus was questioning the nature of creativity. In such an intellectual climate, those susceptible to Rothko's restatement of the old problem of Mallarmé—the absence, the void with its metaphysical echoes—were well equipped. Rothko came, bringing what Rilke called the "suspiration that grows out of silence," and it was understood by those who were listening to the same all but inaudible sounds.

If, as Rothko thought, a picture lives by companionship, there were to be eyes that were prepared to be companionable in Europe. The kind of pictorial thinking Rothko's abstractions represented after 1950 found immediate recognition in Europe in the later 1950s. To some degree, Rothko's thought was itself tempered by the cultural news arriving from Europe. In the early 1950s he saw Motherwell and Philip Guston often—both, artists intensely interested in the way the philosophies being formulated in postwar Europe could enhance their own. Guston was an avid reader and questioner, as was Motherwell. The sources frequently cited by the French writers—Nietzsche, Kierkegaard, Kafka, Dostoyevsky—were already familiar to them, important to them. As these painters stepped out gingerly into the unknown, they looked behind them and they looked forward, scanning the intellectual horizons seeking moral support. It was slow in coming. But they could find confirmation of their daring departures in painting in the respectful attention rendered painting by the most fertile French minds of the postwar era. What they were doing, in the eternal reciprocal round of stylistic choices, could be interpreted comfortably by the European mind that had already moved beyond formalism. Even the most intelligent commentators in America, such as Clement Greenberg, had not yet acknowledged that the kind of "transcendental" experience Rothko posited was possible in painting. Rothko's most serious apologist, and the one he most respected in America, Robert Gold-water, was also loath to admit a metaphysical dimension to pic-torial thought, and insisted in the 1960s that such speculation was "literary fancy."

If there is a context within which Rothko's work may be consid-ered as part of the modern history of thought, it would be found in the peopled silences invoked by a host of French writers from 1945 on—not only philosophers but poets, playwrights, and critics. It would be found in the continuity evident between late 19th-century Symbolism and mid-20th-century Existentialism. It would be found in the resurrection of Nietzsche, especially in France where Gide had first invoked him to support his fin de siècle rebellion against rationalism, and where Sartre and Blanchot would later find impor-tant matter for their definition of the modern spirit. Rothko had ar-rived at his own Nietzschean vision when he spoke of the impossi-bility for the solitary figure to raise its limbs in a single gesture that might indicate its concern with the fact of mortality (1947) and when he said "I belong to a generation in which every artist studied the human figure. It was with the utmost reluctance that I found this figure could not serve my purposes. A time came when none of us could use the figure without mutilating it. If I couldn't find ways of dealing with nature without mutilating it, I felt I had to find other ways to deal with human values" (1958). His personal re-valuation of values was to take the form of a stripping down, a reduction to the pregnant silences already envisioned by the Sym-bolists. Nietzsche thought that "the will loves better to will noth-ingness than not to will." When Nietzsche began his own surpassing effort to separate and rub clean each of his thoughts and words, and to rid himself of meaningless bulk, he took into account the silences from which could arise the purest of thoughts, much as had his con-temporary Mallarmé, and also Rodin, who designated the fragment an emblem of a whole. "The aphorism," Nietzsche wrote, "is a form of eternity; my ambition is to say in ten phrases what another says in a book—does not say in a book." This fanatic thirst for essence would be transmitted in many forms to 20th-century artists. It is the very premise of Existentialism, as Sartre insisted. Subjectivity, he said, must always be the starting point since, in his view, existence precedes essence. The one thing man cannot do is to transcend sub-jectivity. His whole life is a process moving toward essence, which, in effect, is a kind of transcendence. Despite man's solitary situa-tion, he only becomes aware of himself (becomes his essence) through the *cogito* that also perceives all others, and perceives them as a condition of his own existence. Here is the world of "inter-subjectivity" which Rothko anticipated when he spoke repeatedly of the "others" who beheld his pictures, and their "human needs." Rothko was thoroughly prepared, emotionally and intellectually, to consent to the Sartrean vision of art as functioning in the same way as ethics "in that we have creation and invention in both cases. We cannot decide, *a priori* what there is to be done." What Sartre wrote in "Existentialism Is a Humanism," a rather simplified 1945 lecture published as *Existentialism* in New York in 1947, was per-fectly consistent with Nietzsche and what Rothko had assumed from Nietzsche:

> Man is constantly outside of himself; in projecting himself, in losing himself outside of himself, he makes for man's existing; and on the other hand, it is by pursuing transcendent goals that he is able to exist; man, being this state of passing-beyond, and seizing upon things only as they bear upon this passing beyond.

Passing beyond—*outrepasser*—was a key idea found everywhere in the writings meant to interpret the cultural moment that arrived after the Second World War. Beckett, Malraux, Ponge, Camus, Sartre, Blanchot, Merleau-Ponty, Bachelard: all were preoccupied with the word even if, as several of them underlined, it was quite possible that such passing beyond was not possible. Whatever it might mean to individual sensibilities, it had a broad general mean-ing at the time that implied that all is in process at all times, and a part of such process is to transcend the immediate givens of a situa-tion and to understand, as Nietzsche had said, that there are no facts in themselves. Everything is perceived in a situation. Reciprocities are infinite. The readiness of the French thinkers to admit painters into the thinking process was epitomized by Maurice Merleau-Ponty whose writings are permeated with his profound experiences with painting. Merleau-Ponty more than any other postwar writer was able to encompass the acts of the painter in an overall philosophy in

1. *Interior*   c. 1932

2. *Slow Swirl by the Edge of the Sea* 1944

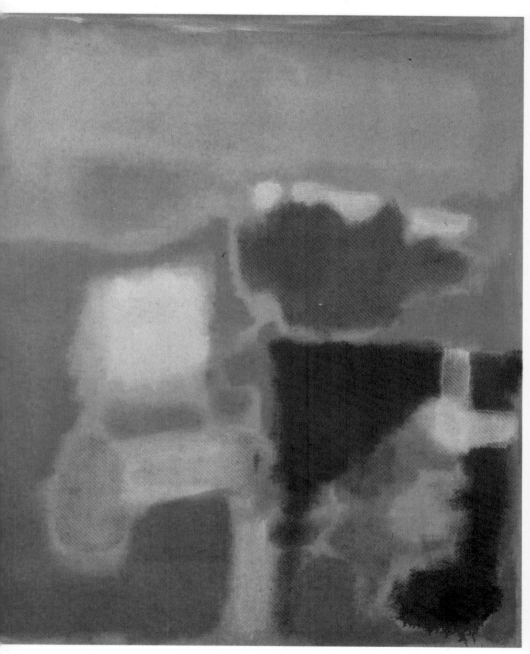

3. *Number 18* 1948–49

4. *Number 18* 1951

5. *Blue over Orange* 1956

6. The Rothko Room at The Tate Gallery, London:
Black on Maroon, 1959; *Red on Maroon*, 1959;
Red on Maroon, 1959

7. *Number 117   1961*

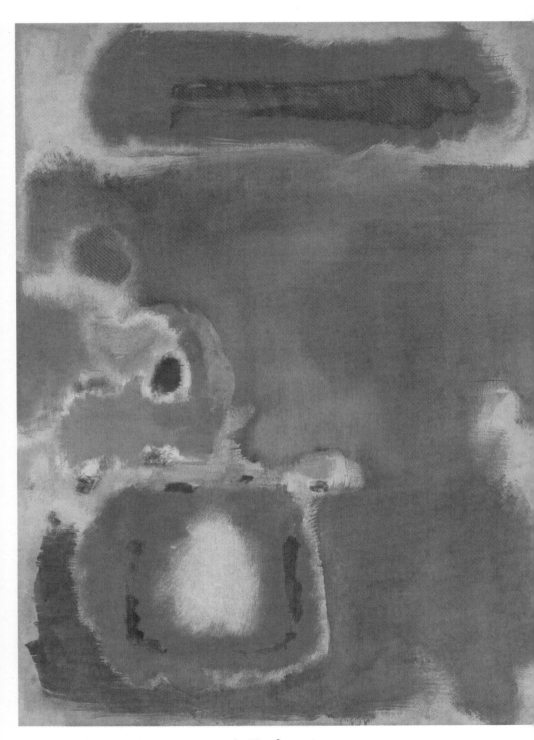

8. *Number 17* 1947

which the language of the painter and the language of the writer were assumed to have common traits. He returned to the great modern tradition born in the genius of Mallarmé and Cézanne in order to understand contemporary art with its implacable will to reduction and aphoristic trenchancy. What Mallarmé understood of language (and his drive to pass beyond it) was its infinite plasticity, its extension into spaces and silences that could not be contained by syntax. He had spoken of two languages: the one he called practical, and the other echoed in the self-mirroring words of his poems. Merleau-Ponty follows Mallarmé:

> Speech in the sense of empirical language—that is, the opportune recollection of a pre-established sign—is not speech in respect to an authentic language. It is, as Mallarmé said, the worn coin placed silently in my hand. True speech, on the contrary—speech which signifies, which finally renders *l'absent de tous les bouquets* present and frees the meaning captive in the thing—is only silence in respect to empirical usage, for it does not go so far as to become a common name.

The passage Merleau-Ponty refers to is in Mallarmé's "Crisis of Poetry":

> If a poem is to be pure, the poet's voice must be stilled and the initiative taken by the words themselves, which will be set in motion as they meet unequally in collision . . . I say: "a flower!" then from that forgetfulness to which my voice consigns all floral form, something different from the usual calyces arises, something all music, essence, and softness: the flower that is absent from all bouquets . . .[43]

The painters are as familiar with this "authentic" language of absence as the poets. There is a tacit language, Merleau-Ponty insists. Both poets and painters speak it and

> We must consider speech before it is spoken, the background of silence without which it would say nothing.

What could be more evident in Rothko's thinking, through his painting? The spaces discerned throughout the poem and the painting are spaces of a modern point of view of existence, spaces that are not outside or inside, but are endemic to all being; spaces, as

Merleau-Ponty says, reckoned only as starting from the individual as the zero point or degree zero of spatiality. On Space:

> I do not see it according to its exterior envelope. I live in it. After all, the world is all around me, not in front of me . . . The question is to make space and light, which are *there,* speak to us.[44]

This he felt Cézanne had done. (Matisse perhaps drew his inferences from Cézanne, for he had stated, in his work and in his explanations of his work, that the space is all around him, "the wall around the window does not create two worlds." And, "Often I put myself into my picture and I am conscious of what exists behind me.") Rothko had arrived through his process at a similar conviction concerning the nature of space, and in 1951 explained that he painted large pictures

> precisely because I want to be very intimate and human. To paint a small picture is to place yourself outside your experience, to look upon an experience as a stereoptic view or with a reducing glass. However you paint the larger picture, you are in it . . .[45]

What the French phenomenologists kept referring to as the "lived" experience was to become Rothko's language, his tacit language, and his pictorial language. As Merleau-Ponty understood (admonishing his readers that there is so much to be learned about thinking from painters), "It makes no difference if he does not paint from 'nature'; he paints, in any case, because he has seen, because the world has at least once emblazoned in him the cipher of the visible."[46]

Painting was Rothko's means, his only means to convey what he called human values that were experienced as a passing beyond; as what older civilizations had called the states of the soul. In order to bring painting to the degree of emotion he had known in music, or in poetry, he had to forgo the naming of things that Mallarmé had consigned to practical language. Henceforth he would attempt to name only his emotions in the grandest, most ardent ways, bearing in mind always the ambivalent situation of modern man. The problem of modern painting, as Rothko had understood, was how to transcend consciousness of self, or, as Merleau-Ponty put it

Modern painting presents a problem completely different from that of the return to the individual: the problem of knowing how one can communicate without the help of a pre-established Nature which all men's senses open upon, the problem of knowing how we are grafted to the universal by that which is most our own.[47]

Rothko in the 1950s was prepared to go beyond Symbolism to sense the silences behind and beneath his every gesture on the canvas. The forms in his paintings would still be like "actors," but now they acted in a different drama in which anecdote disappears into light. The paint would speak, as words would speak in Mallarmé, of other things. He would believe, with Redon, that *"la matière a son genie."* The "lived" experience would be transmitted as directly as possible through paint and he would be, as he early dreamed, the *chef d'orchestre,* and the composer of a great opera like *The Magic Flute:* "Every painting I do now is different, as if I were writing *The Magic Flute*—one day Sarastro, one day Pamina, and so on."[48] In going beyond the symbolism that underscored his work of the late 1940s Rothko ceded to his impatience with practical language, and with the encrusted usages that impaired his vision. He was hearing another sound in the world that pierced to a center. "I know not seems," Hamlet had said.

In 1950, a seasoned painter-turned-art historian, William Seitz, embarked on a thesis that would attempt to explore the foundations of the movement called Abstract Expressionism through examining carefully the works of several artists. He was well liked by his subjects, one of whom was Rothko. Seitz spent many hours in studios, looking and talking. He frequented the artists' cafés and bars and The Club. He compared what was said in one studio with what was said in another. His deep intelligence sifted responses and shaped a picture of the movement that has never been surpassed. Naturally, he had his preferences, and if his work is read closely, Rothko seemed to him to be the most extraordinary of painters (confirmed by Seitz's own painting at the time). Seitz's conversations with Rothko were intense, and although not always directly quoted, inform his view of certain aspects of the movement. In their light, he considers the problem, for instance, of the way American painters approached the notion of the transcendental. Noting their commitment to process, and to the importance of matter itself, Seitz carefully defined the way these artists used the word transcendental to "indicate values, which, though subjective, are not merely personal. They are ideal or spiritual, but still immanent in sensory and psychic experience." He understood Rothko above all to be concerned with such values, and that in his instinctive drive toward an absolute, Rothko was struggling to elicit meanings unmediated by discursive language, or its formal equivalent in painting. Seitz called upon Sartre (and it is probable that he had discussed the passage with Rothko) to help him elucidate:

> Tintoretto did not choose that yellow rift in the sky above Golgotha to *signify* anguish or *provoke* it. It is anguish and yellow sky at the same time. Not sky of anguish or anguished sky; it is an anguish become a thing, an anguish which has turned into yellow rift of sky, and which thereby is submerged and impasted by the proper qualities of things, by their impermeability, and that infinity of relations which they maintain with other things.[49]

Seitz remarks that "Rothko, too, describes his areas as 'things' and like Sartre, emphasizes the 'immanence' of their meaning. Meaning is immanent in the form or, in Sartre's phrase, 'trembles about it like a heat mist'; it *is* color or sound." The passage in Sartre arrested the attention of Merleau-Ponty as well, and he commented that[50] "if we set ourselves to living in the painting, the meaning is much more than a 'heat mist' at the surface of the canvas, since it is capable of demanding *that* color and *that* object in preference to all others, and since it commands the arrangement of a painting just as imperiously as a syntax or a logic. For not all the painting is in those little anguishes or local joys with which it is sown: they are only the components of a total meaning which is less moving, more *legible,* and more enduring." Rothko would have liked this qualification as he was always wary of ecstatic interpretation, although what he sought for himself in his painting was precisely ex-stasis.

All of the clarifying, both in his reveries about painting and in the process of painting, that Rothko undertook around 1949 could not shake his fundamental doubt—a quality inherent in his personality. But it was a new kind of doubt, one focused entirely within the process of painting itself, the kind of doubt Matisse knew when so surprised was he at what had arrived on his canvas that he told a visitor that not he but the postman had painted "The Pink Onions." It was, so to speak, a positive doubt, one that could be turned into energy. Rothko's love of the prefix "trans"—above, over, through, beyond—grew imperious. How many times he had spoken of transformations, transmigrations, transfigurations, transactions, translation!

The "actors" or "things" on the face of his canvas move into place with increasing formality, as though the symmetries of ancient dramas had overcome Rothko's dreams of immemorial creation myths. They float, as in "Number 18" of 1948-49, but in an equilibrium established by near-horizontal balances, and in the apparitional bar— Rothko's familiar reflex to invoke other worlds. The *aura*, never absent from now on, makes its appearance. Boldly he announces his ambiguities. In what he called his "multiform" paintings, reds are moving both inward and to the surface without visible boundaries, and they are nimbused with a pinkish glow, or sent floating behind a rough rectangle of blue. Shapes that are deliberately divested of boundaries, or are pale specters of rectangles, are posited in order to speak of verticality, or of the masking of space by means of light. Memory will speak. The experiences Rothko has known in the act of painting and in his moving from point to point, as he put it, are given their equivalents in reductions to essences. They are remembered in paint. They are spread lightly on the canvas surface, and then overspread. They glimmer or joyously radiate from behind. A manifest preoccupation with what can only be called the apparitional is everywhere (or everywhere and nowhere as Pascal might have said) and recalls the Symbolists' obsessions with murmuring silences. In "Number 11" of 1949, Rothko has recourse to the mirroring symmetries they, the Symbolists, expounded. The bars of whitened blues, reds and pinks that travel upwards on the vertical format are like bars of music, moving toward the climax that is a ghostly rectangle of a whitish-greenish cast containing a pink spectral center, almost an inner eye of the kind Poe anthropomorphized in "The Fall of the House of Usher." These rectangularized shapes disembody the "meanings" known to Rothko in his mythic phase, but they are meanings nonetheless. That is, he has found equivalences to specific feelings of himself in the world and transmits them through stating the paradox: now you see it, now you don't. *Where* is the picture? In the thinnest of membranes covering the threads of the canvas? Hovering before it? Receding behind? In the aura that he sometimes almost literally describes, as when he binds certain works of 1949 with whitish outlines? By 1950, a crucial year for Rothko, these questions were absorbed by an enormous will to work, canvas by canvas, toward transmitting the unnamed passions with which he had lived for so long and for so long sought to express. He had believed, as had the French thinkers, that there was "inter-subjectivity." He could assume that, as he felt the difference between one canvas and the next, so would the onlooker. If he had reduced his composition very nearly to just a few divisions of color, it was color that would be the carrier of mood, of even specific mood. For him, as he always said, each canvas was completely different from the last, despite compositional similarities. For those who, like the phenomenologists, could live in the painting itself, it was not difficult to understand Rothko's elation, or his continuing struggle to make more and more precise the nature of his experience. There were after all other artists attempting a similar enterprise. There was Giacommeti, perhaps the closest parallel, whose quest to locate himself in a space described as "human" brought him to recommence each time with the same configuration, always marveling at how different the nuances of perception can be, and how elusive finally, final definition will be.

Sympathetic viewers such as Thomas B. Hess and William Seitz could find affinities in these new abstractions with certain painters of the past—painters who had attempted, through recapitulating their motifs—to go beyond the given appearances of things. Hess sensitively discerned a Whistlerian sense of space, and Seitz noted that

> Historically, whether or not any influence is involved, Rothko's means might be said to be a continuation of the combination of parallel organization with color films of equivocal depth in Whistler and Monet, though it is a partial or superficial correspondence, for his aims are quite different.[51]

His aims, Seitz felt, always went toward the absolute: "Rothko values the quality of 'immanence,' of a spirit which is indwelling, unified, complete." And, in an indirect quote from Rothko, he designates the Apollonian-Dionysian dualism as the essence of tragic art. "Antitheses, Rothko feels, are neither synthesized nor neutralized in his work but held in a confronted unity which is a momentary stasis." Despite the lush colors of the new works, Rothko had not abandoned his old ideal of "the single tragic idea."

8

"I am still looking for the fabulous," Rothko wrote to the sculptor, Richard Lippold, during his first trip to Europe in the spring of 1950.[52] He had decided to travel to England, France, and Italy with Mell, whose mother had died and left her a small inheritance. Their general economic situation had been poor for several years. Rothko's sales were meager despite his growing reputation. His part-time job at the Brooklyn school could not support them, and he was looking for a job near New York. In his letter he inquires of Lippold about a job in Trenton, New Jersey, and then speaks of his quest for the fabulous, "which they say I will find in Italy." The letter dated May 6, from the French Riviera, hints at Rothko's conflicts. Europe had long represented the spiritual source for Rothko and his friends. But it was also a potential seductress of which the enterprising traveler to the new must be wary:

> I feel like staying put here somewhere for a month or two and making again these things which I am sure few here could have a feeling for: I never realized how really new our world is until I came here.

There were other experiences, though, in Italy, that would subtly invade Rothko's heart and draw him back to Italy twice more in his life. The "really new" had its subsoil of the old, and Rothko was increasingly drawn to it. The fabulous would be found, and not in landscapes but in works of art, much as Rothko often provocatively denied his interest in the work of other artists, particularly other painters, no matter in what century.

Whatever he brought back from that first encounter with Europe (perhaps it was the memory of its architecture; perhaps a first exposure to Fra Angelico, the Thomist enamored of "radiant light everywhere" as Giulio Carlo Argan, an Italian acquaintance of Rothko, would put it), Rothko returned with a reinforced will to surpass. From now on he would court extravagance unabashedly. It is at this point, when he is in his late forties, that he cedes to his will to be ravished. His "enterprise" would take him beyond painting—although painting was his only means—to a point where the *effect* of his painting, just as Mallarmé's effect of words, would be ravishing. What Rothko yearned to possess was some vision of ineluctable beauty that would "tear away," as the word ravish suggests, the uncertainties with which he struggled to the end. The great sensuousness that resided in him and had been so uneasy when attached to things suddenly surged up, when freed of things. His desire to immerse himself (the possibility had been suggested by Nietzsche) in a universe of values rather than things, had found its means. Now Rothko would draw closer to his ideal—the poignancy of music and poetry. The "spirit of music" would inspirit his canvases. He did not forget his Nietzsche. "For if music is really a language of emotion," wrote Susanne Langer, a contemporary of Rothko's, confirming Nietzsche "it expresses primarily the composer's *knowledge of human feelings*, not how or when that knowledge was acquired; as his conversation presumably expresses his knowledge of more tangible things, and usually not his first experience of them."[53] But Rothko was a painter. He had to start again each time to find his first experience of things, without language as mediator.

The boldness of Rothko's address from 1950 on was accompanied by, or perhaps incited by, a stiffening of ethic. If a picture lives by companionship, then companions would have to be carefully chosen. His companion in rebellion, Clyfford Still, was again on the scene in New York when Rothko returned from Europe and the two resumed their old camaraderie. Rothko began to talk of "controlling the situation" and sought to protect his enterprise from the encroachment of a gradually expanding art world, filled with disquieting aspects. Although he would exhibit, once more, in the Whitney Annual of 1950, he was gathering his courage to renounce public exposure in uncontrolled situations such as the untidy mass exhibitions at the Whitney, which asked that Rothko present work to the museum for possible purchase. Declaring that since he had a deep sense of responsibility for the life that his pictures would lead out in the world, Rothko said he would "with gratitude accept any form of their exposition where their life and meaning can be maintained, and avoid all occasion where I feel that this cannot be done . . . at least in my life, I must maintain a congruity between my actions and convictions, if I am to continue to function and do my work." Five years later he reiterated this position to the Whitney's director, Lloyd Goodrich, adding that he understood that he might sound pompous, but asking that his response be seen in the best of faith.

When curator Dorothy Miller chose Rothko together with Baziotes, Pollock, Ferber, Tomlin, and Still, among others, for *Fifteen Americans* in 1952 at the Museum of Modern Art, she found Rothko at first charming and acquiescent. Later he became demanding. He wished to control the installation of his work, even in relation to the others, and he and Still adamantly refused to let their work travel, forcing Miller to cancel plans to circulate the show in Europe. Rothko's unwillingness to appear in group exhibitions, as he told Betty Parsons, was ostensibly because "they just drag you down, while you don't drag them up."[54] Beneath his intransigence, and a need to exercise his will, was an instinct to preserve what he valued most in his work: its potential of enveloping, of drawing the spectator into its ambiance the way Mozart could draw his listeners into his opera in the resounding overtures. Rothko's cultural preoccupations were no less serious and important to him during this period than they had been in his earlier phases. His convictions were essential to his pursuing his work, and he still debated with himself and a few of his colleagues the consequences of his own gestures. During the early 1950s he saw Guston and Motherwell frequently. At times, when he had brooded long enough in his studio, he would set out looking for Guston, who could often be found talking in a few favored bars in the late evenings.

The crucial questions to which Guston and Motherwell addressed themselves in those years of self-definition were questions familiar to Rothko, having to do with the passing-beyond aspect of painting. Both Guston and Motherwell had participated, with a high sense of adventure, in what was felt to be a dismantling of a materialistic tradition going back to the Renaissance. Both had seen the "risk" inherent in painting which turns its back on the named world. Guston was reading intensively: Dostoyevsky, Kafka, Camus above all. Motherwell was preoccupied with Kierkegaard. The conversations these artists had were not about the art world, the world of commodities they so much despised, but about the fate of art itself and the predicament of the artist. The Existentialist bias was evident in a curious obsession on the part of all three of these artists with Kierkegaard's treatment of the parable of Abraham and Isaac. Rothko was accessible to Kierkegaard's argument in his very bones, given his early training and his constant awareness of the great drama in the Old Testament. From Kierkegaard, and from Camus and Sartre with their vision of "authenticity," comes the preoccupation of certain New York School artists with the ethical dimension of painting. Or rather, painting as an ethical act of choice, committed to locating and expressing the deepest of human values. When these artists spoke of "risk" they merely meant to signal their awe inspired by the new conditions with which they confronted themselves in the act of painting. Motherwell would write in his statement for the *New Decade* show at the Whitney in 1955 that pictures are vehicles of passions and not pretty luxuries. "The act of painting is a deep human necessity, not the production of a handmade commodity . . . True painting is a lot more than 'picture making.' A man is neither a decoration nor an anecdote."

The passionate adherence to a philosophical humanism that characterized Rothko and his sympathetic colleagues made it difficult for Rothko to accommodate less romantic visions of the mission of painting. When in 1951 he landed a job at Brooklyn College, where the department harbored a few non-objective artists who took a practical stance in relation to the training of painters in the basic forms of art, Rothko ran into immediate conflict. His deep antipathy for what he summed up as a "Bauhaus" approach emerged. For him there never was and never could be something called "design" that could be taught. All the exercises with pure forms carried out in the Bauhaus tradition (although *not* the tradition maintained there by Klee and Kandinsky) seemed to Rothko futile. His clash with his Brooklyn College colleagues stemmed from his absolute conviction that painting was not apprehended at all if it were apprehended in terms of design. He told Seitz, "One does not paint for design students or historians but for human beings, and the reaction in human terms is the only thing really satisfactory to the artist." When his attitudes at Brooklyn College became too explicit his fellow teachers turned against him, and in 1954 they denied him tenure. At a hearing Rothko defended himself against their accusation that he was not "flexible" enough, and in his notes reconstructing the meeting,[55] set up in question and answer form, he vented his sarcasm. When asked why he was willing to work in a department devoted to an antagonistic philosophy, he answered:

> That is the history of every artist's life. If we awaited for sympathetic environments, our visions which are new would never have to be invented and our convictions never spoken.

When the questioners state that a department is like a team, he answers

> What kind of a team? My idea of a school is Plato's academy, where a man learns by conversing with men of consequence.

This Rothko believed fervently. Years later when he visited Harvard's Carpenter Center, where a Bauhaus approach to design prevailed, he walked silently through a studio full of geometric paper models. Later, when an older European with a well-lived, sympathetic face asked him what he thought, he leaned forward at the luncheon table, with one of his warmest smiles, and answered: "If I were teaching here, I would have them all do your portrait instead." The company laughed. But Rothko was utterly serious.

By the time the upheaval at Brooklyn College took place, Rothko was well set on his course, although he was still in a constricting economic situation. His daughter Kate, born in 1950, would soon have to start school. The loss of a job, even at a time when Rothko's name had already become important in the context of the rise of the New York School, was a serious event, and Rothko was now over fifty, making other teaching jobs less likely. As irritating as he found the situation, Rothko gained something in anger. He worked all the more in his studio and hardened himself increasingly against what he suspected to be a philistinism even in the way the world now seemed to give acceptance to his work. He opposed himself to his time, and even, to some extent, to the movement of which he was said to be a part.

In 1950, Rothko along with seventeen other vanguard artists had signed a letter protesting Metropolitan Museum policies toward contemporary artists, and had posed for a picture for *Life* magazine by Nina Leen—a picture that became famous and that labeled the artists "The Irrascibles." Essentially these artists were the nucleus of the New York School. By the time Elaine de Kooning published her article on Rothko and Kline in *Art News Annual* of 1958, in which she used one of the terms to identify the Abstract Expressionists—Harold Rosenberg's "action painters"—Rothko was ready to separate himself even from his old companions, writing in a letter to the editor that "real identity is incompatible with schools and categories, except by mutilation." Action painting, he said, was antithetical to the very look and spirit of his work.

Rothko felt a kinship with other artists, but was always fiercely concerned with "real identity." Discussions with Motherwell, Guston, Ferber, Stamos, Gottlieb, and many others during the early to mid-1950s seemed always to come back to the problem of preserving the personal integrity of an artist's statement from the wayward interpretations imposed on it by the combined forces that had come to be known as an art world. Rothko was consistently suspicious of institutions, critics, dealers, and the newly established cast of collectors that, by 1955, would be noticed even by *Fortune* magazine in a two-part article (December 1955). It called its readers' attention to the alluring new field for investment—living American artists—and advised its readers to invest in "pioneers," naming Pollock, de Kooning, and Rothko. Rothko felt that the "subject" of his painting was poorly understood, although he had created his own language, a language designed "to avoid doing violence to objects" as he said repeatedly in the 1950s. Watching the expansion of the art world, he felt a profound distaste. "It has degenerated into a free-for-all," he said in 1956, and added bitterly that in America, "one can never become a patriarch, one simply becomes an old man."[56]

If he longed to become a patriarch, the means were at hand, but it was the wrong culture. America's indefatigable quest for the new and the young would thwart him. Rothko sensed, with some accuracy, that his "language" would reach only a few, while his name would reach many. Increasingly he was exasperated with the written responses to his shows. When Katherine Kuh organized an important exhibition at the Art Institute of Chicago in October 1954, he wrote that he abhorred "forewords and explanatory data" because the result is "paralysis of the mind and imagination."[57] When his work was seen not only in America but in an important exhibition *Modern Art in the U.S.A.* that traveled throughout Europe in 1955-56, and in *The New American Painting* that also traveled from 1958 to 1959, he nurtured his skepticism, not allowing himself to believe in his growing fame. Yet, he remained convinced that he could "communicate something about the world" in his new language.

He tried in 1958, for the last time in public, to specify what it was in the human condition, he wished to express. He spoke of the "weight of feelings" and used a musical analogy: Beethoven and Mozart have different weights. He had told Elaine de Kooning shortly before, "I exclude no emotion from being actual and therefore pertinent. I take the liberty to play on any string of my existence."[58] In doing so, Rothko performed difficult feats of thought. Whatever was proposed to him by way of an explanation of what he was doing, and whatever he proposed to himself, was subjected to endless scrutiny. None of the conventional approaches to painting could satisfy his vision. He disclaimed an interest in color, although color, he conceded, had remained his only means. "Since there is no line, what is there left to paint with?" he told Elaine de Kooning, adding that color "was merely an instrument." When he was called a colorist, he angrily disclaimed it, pointing out that colorists are interested in arrangements, while as soon as he saw his own painting as an arrangement, "it has to be scrapped." When asked about space he was similarly recalcitrant. Space, he insisted to Seitz, like color or flatness, is not essential to his conception. "He

134

emphasizes the material facts: that his variously shaped color areas are simple 'things' placed on a surface." Years later, in 1961, he told a reporter: "In our inheritance we have space, a box in which things are going on. In my work there is no box: I do not work with space. There is a form without the box, and possibly a more convincing kind of form."[59]

In all his statements Rothko was trying to find a verbal context for what he ultimately felt to be inexpressible in words—his consuming love for the virtual which urged him again and again to make a sign that would at once be, and not be. He would repeat the Existentialist notion that, as he put it, "a painting is not about experience, it is an experience." The nature of the experience, of course, had to be in space. What else could a painter qualify? But these virtual spaces he dreamed had different qualifications. Basically Rothko had to assume that there was a space in which others and he could commune. Otherwise, what could a painting mean? Yet it had to be a material fact, "things" on surfaces. If he could submerge himself, and the others, in the spaces he created, the spaces would no longer be virtual. The painting would no longer "seem" but would "be." And yet, it would have the spectral presence that is literally neither here nor there.

Rothko had to assign values, and often his viewers were skeptical. In 1956 when he still worked in a cramped room and could never have more than one or two of his large canvases visible, he used to keep one of his earliest huge abstractions, "Number 22," 1949, against a wall in a narrow storage area. This early essay into a kind of limitless space, with huge areas of floating yellow and orange, interrupted only by a red band straddling the canvas from side to side, shocked unaccustomed eyes. Rothko had not quite reached the ambiguity he would shortly perfect and, to call attention to the picture plane and its function as the final determinant of image, he had scored the rectangular red form with scraped lines. This painting, he said, with its large area of yellow and its bright red was perceived by most people as optimistic. But, he emphasized, "it is tragedy instead." He had assigned a value which in time would come to be understood, but not by everyone. The painting, by its scale alone, could be an equivalent to an epic drama. The eye is given a

24. *Number 22* 1949

desert of yellow in which to wander, perhaps with anxiety, until it reached a narrow border of still paler yellow which with its fading edges is not even really a border. The very time it takes to reach a visual resting point in scanning such a canvas is enough to endow it with faintly disturbing qualities that Rothko could see in terms of tragedy. For him, clearly, the "things," the roughly rectangular shapes moving now slightly forward and now back, were, as he said, actors enacting events in which there were unnamable feelings that would find a resolution on the surface of his canvas.

There were the shadowy whispers behind the final surface, speaking of hidden events (for Rothko admitted, with irony, that his paintings *were* façades, as Elaine de Kooning had suggested). The source of light was skillfully concealed, so that the scanning eye could never be quite sure. Here was a yellow surface, but beneath was Rothko's familiar *vibrato* giving the surface an immaterial visage, a feeling of virtuality. Even yellow, with its conventional association with sunlight, would undergo Rothko's transformation of meaning. It, too, partook of a long harbored and enormously refined love of chiaroscuro. It was Rothko's portion to take what was most moving about the love of light in the painterly tradition. He had been moved not only by Fra Angelico, but by Rembrandt. He would smuggle the great tradition into the 20th century. Where there is a plane in his works of the 1950s there is also a shadow. In each case there would be an underpainting meant to be sensed as shadow, and an oscillating surface meant to be sensed as light. To enhance luminosity, Rothko often resorted to the methods of the old masters. He liked to use tempera, which he concocted with fresh eggs, as a base. When he insisted that it was not color that interested him, Rothko was not being arbitrary, for what he meant was to create light, generate light by overpainting, masking, thinning, and thickening, and working for the musical effect, the *vibrato* to which he responded in the most poignant of Mozart's late works. Reaching for these rare effects, Rothko managed to invent juxtapositions of colored surfaces that had no precedent. Robert Motherwell thought that:

> Rothko's mixture resulted in a series of glowing color structures that have no exact parallel in modern art, that in the profoundest sense of Baudelaire's invocation to modern artists, are *new*. So

new that if Rothko had not existed, we would not even know of certain color possibilities in modern art. This is a technical accomplishment of magnitude. But Rothko's real genius was that out of color he had created a language of feeling.[60]

Motherwell accurately described Rothko's spirit as "a certain colored despair that nevertheless glowed with an inner luminosity of color that is a 'poignant' occasion—to employ one of his favored terms." The language of feeling which Rothko developed through the weighing out of measures of color intensities was far from the demotic language, and depended as much on an occult vision of shadows as it did on light.

These masked chiaroscuro effects unavoidably established moods to which Rothko would give their "weight." In the 1953 "Number 61" Rothko takes his large canvas and fills it so that it brims with presences that seem to inhabit different spaces. As in many of his later works, he weights the painting at the top by placing the brushed, scumbled brownish-red over a blue ground. It is read as both density and transparency, but basically, it is read as a darkness against which the scraped and airy blue horizontal beneath it plays, opening out into an azure of infinity and seeping into the darker blue below. These weighted and delicately balanced densities are replete and, in filling the canvas, have a kind of lyrical grandeur. But in another painting keyed to blue, "Whites and Greens in Blue" (1957), the feeling is utterly different. There is little exuberance here. Rather, gravity. Fate. The three forms lying on a blue ground have a kind of finality. The murmuring underpainting is controlled, held within the tightly organized central scheme in which Rothko suggests impingement, but barely. At the time this painting was completed, Rothko claimed that he was creating the most violent painting in America. When I visited him during 1956 and 1957, he always brought the subject up, without offering further elucidation. I took it to mean that by a supreme effort of will he had harnessed turbulence and was painting the paradox of violence; that the colors that produced immeasurable tensions among themselves were conceived as symbols. They had been a thousand times refined, and all smudgy echoes of the everyday world had been removed, but for him, and then for me, they were equivalents of complex emotions.

Lightness and darkness, yes. But not color with any conventional designation of meaning. What could it mean, for instance, when he placed a large horizontal of dark blue over a red-orange ground, as in "Blue Over Orange" of 1956? The burning red is all but blotted out by the depth of the blue, but then, it is modified. Above, the red surround is fierce, below, where it is given back to the sun and is a pale orange expanse, it is almost tender. The brush strokes soften contours; ravel their edges, and at the same time, paradoxically, give a certain relief quality to the form. In the same year Rothko painted "Brown, Black on Maroon," with an entirely different "weight" of feeling. When he moved to the darker register, it was inevitable that the tragic associations so important to him were invoked. The chiaroscuro is heightened. A whole drama seems to be taking place behind the thinly disguised upper register which is pushed into a recessive position by the brilliant shivering band of scarlet light beneath it. The largest form—the black made so rich in its thinly layered overpaintings—then comes forward, an emphatic "thing" with a weight and stability that cannot be altered by the flickering reds of its nimbus.

The suggestion of aureole is not exaggerated. Many of Rothko's paintings recall his earlier obsession with the aura—the subtle, invisible emanation or exhalation; that cloud of air that hung about the gods. In the 1940s he was already endeavoring to paint the suspended, infinitely extensible air that hung about his mythic visions. If he was to find the doorway of which he spoke, leading beyond the everyday, he would need to be able to conjure his aura. The idea of an aura is precisely that it must be more than perceived. Paradox is in its nature. All perception is paradoxical since we can never be sure that we have "seen" all that is there, and in some way we select aspects that are forever changing as we see them, as Cézanne discovered. If our habit is always to carry such a paradox in mind, we will, almost by reflex—a *cultured* reflex—perceive this aura even when we are not in its presence. Rothko was right to count on our perceptual culture. For us, his auras can be like music in that we carry with us the after-image of his generalized auras. He said he wanted to hold things in suspension. He wanted to maintain both the immediate experience (which he called materiality) and

25. *Number 27*   1954

its description, which necessarily moves away from it. For this he invoked another paradox, which is that of time. His painting was to be immediately perceived, and yet, to unfold its communication in time. Light from outside would slowly reveal the light within. A slow rhythm of apprehension would be established. Those whites which Rothko had made into a material thing, having the weight and value of color, were to serve as metaphors for the passing-beyond of the thing, but they were also the thing. In 1951 he painted "Number 18," an immensely bold image in which a great plane of dense white rivets our attention and then, slowly, filters out into the reddish edge, as though it were given, only to be dissipated. Its shadow lies below, mitigated by the hints of modeling in its horizontal bar that suggests how near the ideal blankness the form above has come. This reciprocity is always present in Rothko's paintings of auras and it is wedded to the question of metaphor in painting. It is never light—that ever-vanishing virtuality—as in the sky over the sea, because it is material, it is paint. But it is also a most precise metaphor of such light. At times Rothko went further with a romantic vision of aura and specter, as in the 1954 "Number 27" in which the aura itself has an aura, and all things are doubled and mirrored, with whites beneath the central white. The reversibility or reciprocity here is provided by Rothko's thin technique which allows darker shapes to read as light and the white to read as a denser substance—some ghostly reminder of another place, perhaps the place in which Rothko once said he could breathe and stretch his arms.

These works of the 1950s leading up to the mural cycles were often very large, not, as Rothko said, with the intention of monumentality but with the intention of intimacy. He was still a Nietzschean. He wished for himself, and by extension, for his viewers, an experience of dissolution into a whole not unlike Nietzsche's; also not unlike Mallarmé's who had said toward the end of his life that the sole duty of the poet was to give an Orphic explanation of the universe. The Orphic is dramatic by the very nature of the myth of Orpheus and sometimes, in these large expanses with their grand curtains of darkness, as in "Number 128 Blackish Green on Blue" (1957), Rothko sounds his strongest intimations of origins. There is

26. *Number 9*   1958

a silence here, the kind of silence Melville called "the general consecration of the universe." In "Number 9" (1958), with its play on hues of red—darkened with browns in one register, heightened to the pitch of fire in another—Rothko offers in his tacit language an equivalent to a complex of emotions that can be likened, as he knew, only to the equivalents produced by poets and composers.

The music analogy, or rather, the concern with the "spirit of music," was simply a way for Rothko to deal with the unprecedented nature of his enterprise. He sought out musicians and he was friendly with several composers, among them Morton Feldman with whom he used to visit the Metropolitan Museum. Feldman maintained relations with several painters in the Abstract Expressionist group, and was always a willing and demonstrative viewer. His own work in the 1950s was characterized by his friend and sometimes mentor, John Cage, who offered in The Club in 1949 "A Lecture on Something." With his usual mystification, Cage had called attention to the sense of void typical of Feldman's work of the 1950s. "When nothing is securely possessed one is free to accept any of the some-things," Cage said. "It is quite useless in this situation for anyone to say Feldman's work is good or not good. It is."[61] He added that Feldman's music "continues" rather than changes. In the same sense, Rothko's paintings of the 1950s continued, with each canvas expressing in its tacit language an aspect of his vision of the entire human drama; of the single idea that would represent all the ideas of human feelings.

9

When Rothko made his last public statement, on October 27, 1958, in an old classroom at Pratt Institute, he began speaking without his notes. He spoke haltingly in a quiet voice about what it meant to be an artist, pointing out that he had begun relatively late in life, and that he had formed a speaking vocabulary long before he had formed a painting vocabulary. It was easier to paint pictures than to talk about them, he thought, but still, talk was necessary. He issued a rebuke to Expressionists who "strip themselves of will, of intelligence, of the bonds of civilization" and who seemed not to understand that "painting a picture is not a form of self-expression. Painting, like every other art, is a language by which you communicate something about the world."[62] The dictum "Know thyself" is only valuable he said, if the ego is removed from the process in search for truth. Not surprisingly, he invoked Kierkegaard's *Fear and Trembling.* He had pondered the parable of Abraham and Isaac for years, and frequently in conversations with friends had cited it, for he was seriously engaged, as had been Kierkegaard, in unraveling the meaning of that Old Testament horror story.

Rothko's thoughts on the Kierkegaard interpretation of the Old Testament story went something like this: Kierkegaard is describing the artist. Abraham is called upon to commit "a unique act which society cannot condone." Abraham is caught between the universal law and the law that governs the individual conscience (much as the heroes of Rothko's other admired source, Aeschylus, had been). The artist—that is, Rothko—is compelled to sacrifice, to commit a unique act, as all artists must, even if it comes into conflict with the universal law. Behind this interpretation lay the tacit hope of retrieval, even redemption. It is not too much to talk about "faith" when speaking of Rothko, as skeptical as he sometimes wished to appear, as modern as he professed to be, as detached as he claimed he was. "The fact is," Kierkegaard had written, "the ethical expression for what Abraham did is that he wanted to murder Isaac; the religious, that he wanted to sacrifice him. But precisely in this contradiction is contained the fear that may well rob one of one's sleep." Rothko, as close friends knew, was the victim of robbery almost nightly. The ethical imperatives of his youth gave him no peace. Old friends remember the animated arguments of the 1930s when Rothko would pose the Dostoyevskian dilemma, asking—for instance—if there were a fire, and in the house was a child and a Rembrandt, which would you save? His answer was always a passionate "The child! No painting is worth human life." His dwelling in the moral realm gave him no peace. (Once we enter this realm in which Rothko spent much of his time, there can be nothing but difficulty. Kierkegaard says as much in his *In Vino Veritas*, arguing that the "loveable" cannot be defined. He finds his interlocutor's position untenable since "it contains a double contradiction—first, that it ends with the *inexplicable*, second that it *ends* with the inexplicable; for he who intends to end with the inexplicable, had best begin with the inexplicable and say no more, lest he lay himself open to suspicion. If he begins with the inexplicable, saying no more, then this does not prove his helplessness, for it, anyway, is an explanation in a negative sense; but if he does begin with something else and lands in the inexplicable, then this certainly does prove his helplessness.")

In Kierkegaard's sense, Rothko's was a religious enterprise, with the sacrifice and attendent violence. There was always the helplessness before the inexplicable, and the uneasiness in the interpreted world. Still, Rothko could dream of the symmetries and grand dramas of the ancients, and once again, passed beyond the contingent when he stressed in the 1958 lecture going beyond individual ego. Art is not self-expression, as he had thought in his youth. The notion of schools of art stems from an idea of self-expression that regards the activity of painting as a process in itself, he said. But he could not accept that. "A work of art is another thing." The notion of self-expression, he said, was proper to the vanity of a beautiful woman or a monster, but not an artist. "For an artist, the problem is to talk about and to something outside yourself."

For several years Rothko had been moving toward the views he expressed in the Pratt lecture. His desire to immerse himself in the spaces his paintings proposed became more and more imperious until it occurred to him that the most satisfying means would be the most literal: that canvases would surround the viewer as murals. Fortunately the opportunity to move into the larger scheme—what he called the "jointed scheme"—arrived in the form of an invitation by Philip Johnson to paint murals for the Four Seasons Restaurant in the Seagram Building. Rothko was spurred to find a large studio, a former YMCA gymnasium at 222 Bowery, which he set up in the spring of 1958. The following spring he set out for Europe, where he was well known thanks to the exhibition of his work in the previous year's Venice Biennale. He was treated like a king, as he later reported, and he obviously enjoyed the affectionate attention he received in Italy. By the time he got to Rome, where old friends such as Toti Scialoja and Gabriella Drudi were awaiting him, Rothko was in high spirits, eager to look about him, talk, meet people, and seek experiences with artists of the past. They visited the oldest churches in Rome, and drove out to Tarquinia to see the Etruscan murals resplendent with the colors that Rothko loved best. The scale of the chambers in which the Etruscan painters had so elegantly praised life was the human scale that Rothko often spoke about, having little to do with literal size (the rooms are small) but with the way experience is presented, without hyperbole and heroics. In Rome itself, Rothko wandered about with his friends, taking in the horizontal architecture and discussing its unique charms. His interest in architecture, as Drudi says, was greater than most people thought. When the Scialojas had visited New York two years before, Rothko had taken them almost at once to see the Sullivan building that few ever bother to visit in downtown New York.

One of the most significant events during that important trip to Italy was a visit to Paestum and Pompeii. As a frequent visitor to the first floor of the Metropolitan Museum, Rothko had long been moved by the Greco-Roman vision. But the visit to the actual sites was immensely moving to him. He spoke of it many times to friends, and John Fisher, an editor of *Harper's* magazine who had met Rothko on the ship going to Europe, and again on the trip to Pompeii and Paestum, captured some of Rothko's excitement in his account.[63] At Paestum, a remarkable site where the Greeks had built a majestic Doric temple whose columns still bespeak its singular beauty, he was asked by some Italian tourists if he had come to paint the temple. "I have been painting Greek temples all my life without knowing it," Rothko replied. Fisher also mentions that Rothko found "affinities" in the House of Mysteries in Pompeii— affinities he had already experienced at the Metropolitan Museum with the wall paintings of Boscoreale. It was during this second sojourn in Italy that Rothko again visited Florence, where he saw two important monuments with a different eye. The first is Michelangelo's Laurentian Library with its sense of closure; its stairwell surmounted by blind windows, its corridors hermetic, as was suitable for a monastic library. Fisher mentions Rothko's allusion to Michelangelo's walls in the staircase room in the Medicean Library. A few months later Rothko spoke of the corridor of the Laurentian Library which he felt had lingered in his memory as he worked on the Seagram murals. The corridor, with its insistence on enclosing the presence moving through it, was a likely metaphor for Rothko who, even before the murals, talked always of "controlling the situation."

The other important experience in Florence was Fra Angelico's murals in the Convent of San Marco. Rothko's apprehension of Fra Angelico was not casual. When he was moved, he could be very thorough in exploring the causes for his emotions. In Italy, he not only spent careful hours perusing Fra Angelico's works, but he also discussed the painter with one of Italy's most acute art critics and historians, Giulio Carlo Argan, who had recently written a monograph on Fra Angelico. This painter was to remain a beacon for Rothko. He would return to San Marco during his last Italian journey in 1966. It is not a matter of "influence" or even temperamental affinity. Fra Angelico was important to Rothko because Rothko understood the context within which he functioned, and because he himself had shifted his sights. His aesthetic was now a renunciation of self-expression in favor of meditation. His innate Platonism had triumphed over the tumultuous emotion that had once governed his works. Quite possibly Argan's interpretation of Fra Angelico's unique situation in 15th-century Italy helped Rothko resolve his point of view as he embarked on his most important artistic adventures—the mural cycles of the late 1950s and 1960s. Argan traces Fra Angelico's painting career, stressing always that he was a churchman and theologian who rose in the Dominican ranks and who was attuned to intellectual values. He was not the naïve, rapturous, and angelic figure of mythic art history. Rather, he expressed his point of view through "the purely theoretical values he attached to light."[64] In the beginning, Fra Angelico took a middle position betwen the two views prevailing in his time. Cennino Cennini, whose views often reflected medieval studio practises, maintained that painting was "the art of eliciting unseen things hidden in the shadow of natural ones . . . and serving to demonstrate as real the things that are not." Leon Battista Alberti, a modern humanist with a scientific bias, maintained that "invisible things cannot be said to come within the painter's compass and he seeks only to depict what he sees." Fra Angelico's mission, as a Dominican monk, was to depict what he saw in nature in the light of its unseen source, God. He and his order were resolute Thomists. When Fra Angelico painted his scenes of Edenic beauty, he was true to the Thomist vision of Beauty as "that in which the eye delights," but he acknowledged the Thomist principle that painting is knowledge as "it satisfies our desire to understand and know." For the Thomists, the world and its beauties could be depicted only as effects for which there could be only one cause. God would be the source of all visual pleasure, and the light that would grace the world of nature would always flow from Him. Therefore, in Fra Angelico's exemplary panels, the light is evenly distributed, not modified by Alberti's new principles of perspective, which Fra Angelico used intermittently for his own purposes.

The teachings of Blessed Giovanni Dominici lay behind Fra Angelico's mission. Dominici had laid the groundwork for Fra Angelico's order in his approach to nature as tangible proof of God's goodness. He reasoned that if we are to contemplate God, we must scale the ladder of logic from effects to causes; indeed, to the prime and unique cause where at last, "the thirsty intellect is quenched" and the order of the natural world expands to the universal order of the heavenly hierarchy:

> Here are the rejoicing of angels and apostles, the dancing of martyrs and confessors, the choir of virgins, the joys of all elect. Here are the true sun, the morning star, the flower of the lofty field, the lily of the valley of the just, the rose that never fades, the violet that never withers, carnations, cinnamon and balsam, with the most fragrant perfumes of the Kingdom of the Blessed. Every pleasure has its source in God. There is no pleasure that comes not from Him. How foolish is he who seeks pleasure elsewhere![65]

Many of Fra Angelico's resplendent middle-period works are seemingly illustrations of Dominici's lyrical instructions. Light would be the binding vehicle of meaning, making all the objects and figures instinct with its source. As Argan writes, "Fra Angelico posited light on the qualitative principle by which human experience, limited in scope and heavy with 'quantity' might be sublimated into a supreme ideal of being."

But these altarpieces and predellas in which Fra Angelico lavished heavy pigments, literally jewel-like, as when he uses large amounts of lapis lazuli, and in which there are many allusions to nature, are different from the frescoes that so moved Rothko in the Convent of San Marco. Here, Fra Angelico divested himself of the world with its cheerful colored substances. He sacrificed the lapidary beauty of heavy pigment. Instead, he moved to sober transparencies in which there are only traces of the past splendor in which he had decked the world. These murals in the cells of monks and in the cell of their patron, Cosimo de Medici, are not meant to edify or cajole. There can be only one reason for their existence: to assist the monk in his ritual of contemplation and prayer—activities that can lead to rapture, but only within the monastic walls. Argan remarks on "the thoroughness with which, at San Marco, history, nature and myth have been ruled out in favor of rite and symbol." Fra Angelico limits his themes, using the symbols of Christ's Passion sparingly. He scales down his colors to their faintest values, taking advantage of the soft white ground of fresco to lend an evenly flowing, unnaturally pale light that emanates from no solid source and illuminates no solid body. Everything in these works is reduced to its purest essence, and often there are whitenesses that bespeak a totally unearthly experience. There is no given space here, no space that can be likened to perspectival perception. The single figures are consumed by the cool flowing light as are incidental details—a briefly sketched hill or tree, or a blue ground that cannot even be perceived as sky, so much has it become a symbol for something other. Anyone moving from cell to cell in San Marco would be struck by the evanescence, the immateriality of the scenes depicted, and by the way Fra Angelico conjures a space that knows no limits and yet flows tangibly before one's eyes. The surprising note of tragedy in the sober transparencies and the starkness of presentation are also sustained, as though Fra Angelico, among his peers, allowed himself to speak of another kind of human experience—the despair of the individual seeking his moment of enlightenment; the moment to slake his intellectual and spiritual thirst. Rothko, moving from cell to cell, and feeling the immense emotional investment of this monk who was able to sustain the sanctified atmosphere throughout the large monastery with a stark simplicity of means, felt an emotional affinity that would express itself shortly after in his own mural cycles. He certainly retained the impression left by the large "Crucifixion" in the main hall. Here the three crosses are stark and mournful against a rust, or dried-blood red sky (possibly originally meant only as a ground for lapis-lazuli), and the semicircular composition falls into three bands of light. Practised as he was at seeing the grand scheme over the narrative, Rothko was moved by the austere power of this work.

At the time he was working arduously on the Seagram commission, he was having an intense debate with himself about the meaning of art. He sought out friends who themselves were given to searching questions. There were long philosophical evenings. One of his most stimulating associations was with the poet Stanley Kunitz, who saw Rothko at the time as "a primitive, a shaman who finds the magic formula and leads people to it."[66] Kunitz wrote about poetry during that period that "it is not concerned with communication; it has its roots in magic, incantation, and spell-casting." Kunitz shared Rothko's vision of the contemporary world as fraught with distressing problems, believing, as he said in a public lecture in 1959, "we do not have a steady gaze on a fixed reality."[67] The great work of man, Kunitz felt, is "to set up a world of values to shore himself against the ruinous dissolution of the natural world." He and Rothko had often discussed the moral dimension in poetry and painting. Kunitz saw a danger in the generalizing tendency of abstract painting, quoting Blake's admonition to pay attention to "minute particulars" and Hölderlin's belief that nobility in art lies not in the noble but in the commonplace. Rothko, who had always maintained that he was no mystic but a materialist, warmed to the argument, defending his move away from objects. Kunitz's position was never far from Rothko's, for he posited the ethical as the very core of poetry. "In the best painting," he said, "as in authentic poetry, one is aware of moral pressures exerted; an effort to seek unity in the variety of experience. Choices are important. Moral pressure exists to make right and wrong choices." Even more, he felt, as did Rothko, that "all failures are pardonable except the failure of conscience." They agreed that art constitutes a moral universe. As Kunitz put it: "The world is defended by art, made more livable because art does deal with pleasure. It gives us the image of Eden, the idea, the beautiful. Art, by setting up the ideal makes man discontented with less than the ideal." In an even more specific statement, suggesting deep affinities with Rothko's views, Kunitz wrote in a letter:

> My predilection, however, is clear enough—it's for Insight that subsumes Sight, for Vision that annihilates Taste. The only worlds that count (or do I mean Words?) are self-contained universes. Adam became the father of poetry when he gave names to the beasts of the field. But it was Noah, when he admitted them two by two to the ark, who became the first critic.[68]

Such convictions stated from many sides in the wandering conversations between painter and poet fed into Rothko's enterprise. They gave him the breathing space, the passing-beyond the petty trivialities of day-to-day art world preoccupations, and the confirma-

27. Untitled   c.1944-46

152

tion of his intuitions. Moreover, Kunitz was attuned to the larger philosophical issues of the postwar period, the issues so avidly discussed in Europe but less often examined in the United States. Years later, Kunitz would look back on his experience with Rothko's work and say that he was moved by its grandeur, its rhetoric of color. "I felt definite affinities between his work and a kind of secrecy that lurks in every poem—an emanation that comes only from language." This restatement of the old dream—the Mallarméan ideal—if uttered, as it surely had been, during the discussions between Rothko and Kunitz, could console Rothko in his task; a task that he labored with incessantly. It is not incidental that Rothko produced several cycles for the Seagram commission, seeking always to capture the "emanation" that for him could come only from paint.

Rothko prepared himself for his task by returning to a medium he had found responsive so many years before. He made a number of gouache sketches in which he allowed himself sensuous play with color, and in which he experimented with sequences of shapes that implied a third dimension more emphatically than his recent large paintings. Some of these sketches initiated a movement on lateral lines, climaxed by images of fiery doorways. Some had bright blue gateways to a relatively atmospheric ground. In some there were yellows and crimsons, and flares of flame blue. It was evident that he was bent on moving beyond the stately containments of his last large paintings, imagining perhaps a "corridor" of corridors through which his viewers would enter Rothko's universe. These initial pictorial ideas with their occasional swelling forms; their clear preoccupation with rousing the senses, and their departure from the symmetries of his earlier abstractions would go through many transformations as Rothko ordered and re-ordered his processional forms. The sequence of his procedures would be, as he had said years before, toward clarity—a clarity he felt he had achieved only after dozens of essays.

In the first series, Rothko stayed close to his sketches, using color contrasts and forms freed from rectilinearity. He stressed vertical elements, no doubt because of the architectural nature of this enterprise. Perhaps the association so many have had with portals on seeing these forms is well-founded. Originally, the dining room graced with an entire long wall of his murals, was to have been seen from an adjoining employees' dining room through large doors. He worked painting by painting, holding in his imagination the effect he wished to receive when they would finally find their form as an ensemble. He had often spoken of his life's work as an ellipse, or sometimes as an oval. It was characteristic of him to think of beginnings and endings as consecrated moments, and his insistence in 1958 in his Pratt lecture that the artist must have a "clear preoccupation with death" and that "all art deals with intimations of mortality" and that "tragic art, romantic art deals with the fact of man born to die" would play its part in these and subsequent mural cycles. Rothko painted, canvas by canvas, a cycle in which the parts would take their place in an imaginary space that he carried about in his mind's eye, and only later in the place they were meant to embellish. (The fact is that none of the "places" allocated for his mural cycles was ever quite satisfactory, and perhaps none could ever be, given Rothko's peculiar fusion of architectural tact and painterly individualism.)

As Rothko worked his way into the second cycle, bringing back with him his memory of experiences in Italy, he strengthened his allusions to post and lintel. The reds and blacks of Pompeii seemed to haunt him. Yet, he meant to talk about human respiration: an organic softness sometimes invaded the rectangular shapes. They hover, trembling, and sometimes seem on the verge of collapse. The original essays in gouache are remembered in the brushwork that in the murals often takes on an expressive function, enlivening or quieting surfaces. His animistic approach at times led to the formation of two entities huddling together. Sometimes there are darkling canvases in which the artist clearly sought to suggest black mysteries behind the final plane of his canvas. The implication of a third dimension is always there, and there were, in several of the paintings of the second cycle, interior auras: there would be the gate-like vertical form in the central recess and within that, a tympanum of shadow.

In the spring of 1958, I had made one of my periodic visits to the studio and Rothko talked again about "controlling the situation." By "situation" he meant many things. He meant to reinvoke his ethical position announced in the early 1940s. He meant, literally, situation—*where* things are situated and *how* they are to be perceived. With the mural commission, his "jointed scheme" would control the situation, although paradoxically, as he had once pointed out, the large canvases take you into them, you are not outside of them, "it isn't something you command."[69] By 1959, he was deeply immersed in the problem of making his scheme conform to his inner vision, working indefatigably. In October 1959, I again visited the cavernous studio with its deep-dyed red floor. Rothko had no lights on, and the great space was dim as a cathedral. When a tiny white cat sprang into the center of the room it was a shock. I felt as though I had walked into a theater, or into an ancient library. The only perceptible object in the huge space was a table, very small in its isolation. Rothko watched my reaction as I examined the arrangement of large canvases and said, "I have made a place." For me it was a place like Tintoretto's place in Venice when I had first seen it, with all the large paintings sunk in darkness so that I would never forget their presences. The paintings I saw that day included a deep maroon with a collapsing crimson rectangle that seemed to sway like a censer in its ambiguous space. At the end of a sequence that Rothko had arranged that day for my visit, a painting with an orange-red slit in an oxblood matrix reminded me of a shape of a Renaissance fortification, or shapes in the Japanese Noh theater. It was a long visit, with intermittent conversation, and at the end, as I was taking my leave, Rothko said: "They are not pictures."

In an important sense Rothko was right. They are not pictures. They are not icons either. They are images, however, if by image we mean that which is thrown upon the imagination and cannot be expunged. Painting was Rothko's only means, but the image was his vision, and who, even the painter himself, can define a man's vision? In the murals Rothko's frankly theatrical use of fiery reds, with their climax of pure pigment, moving with the flickering unevenness of candlelight invokes the blood and fire purification of old ritual. The burning quality was heightened deliberately as Rothko mixed raw pigments into the final surfaces of these canvases. The undeniably portal-like or window-like shapes are not the stony portals of real architecture, but rather the vanishing, never-to-be entered portals of the Old Testament—the Law, the Law as Kafka described in his memorable allusions to portals. The study of proportions in Rothko's mural cycles, which was one of his deepest interests, was not so much rooted in the practical needs of the Seagram restaurant as in Rothko's need to understand the abstract notion of proportion as he might have encountered it in Aeschylus.

These paintings had to respond to an inner vision that could never be quite satisfied in actual *situ*, as confirmed by Rothko's eventual refusal to deliver them. Various reasons have been offered, including his indignation that the original plan to have employees see the works was thwarted when it was decided to change the architecture. More likely Rothko had installed his works in an interior theater of his own with which no real place would ever compare. The history of that last cycle bears that out. When Sir Norman Reid, Director of the Tate Gallery, visited Rothko in 1965 with the proposal that a special room be allocated in the Tate for his work, Rothko saw another opportunity to "control the situation." He rejected Reid's proposal that he give a "representative" group of paintings, offering instead a group of the Seagram murals. He had great difficulty, however, making up his mind, and the negotiations went on for years. Rothko went to London in 1966 to see the space, and, as Reid reported, "like Giacometti," who had also been offered a room, "he admired the scale of the rooms and the light, which can be particularly beautiful."[70] When he returned to New York he wrote to Reid:

> It seems to me that the heart of the matter, at least for the present is how to give this space you propose the greatest eloquence and poignancy of which my pictures are capable. It would help a great deal if there exists a plan which you could send me. I could then think in terms of a real situation and it would make something concrete, at least for me.[71]

After his serious illness in 1968, Rothko wrote Reid that he had had to neglect many things, but that "I still hold the room at the Tate as part of my dreams." He was concerned with every detail and after all was arranged, sent Reid a swatch of the color of his own studio walls so that everything could be exactly as Rothko had worked it out for himself. He had also indicated to Reid that he wished to hang his work in the older section of the museum, near the Turners. Eventually, the nine paintings were hung after his death in a room adjacent to Giacometti's room.

When the Tate paintings are viewed as an ensemble, it is possible to see that Rothko's "jointed scheme" with its ambitious intention of enveloping artist and viewer in a suite of related moods is not entirely without precedent, and that Rothko has moved within a tradition that has already conditioned both the artist and his viewer. The necessity of reciprocity was essential in Rothko's way of thinking about his mural enterprise. If he moved one canvas into a relationship, and then substituted another, it was not that he had no real mural intention. Rather, he sought the enveloping sensation that can be generated when tones from one surface echo another; when the events on the canvas have the psychological effect of drawing the viewer into its space, rather than allowing him to stand outside, as did the Renaissance artists. This almost metaphysical notion of reciprocity, celebrated in the works of the Symbolists at the end of the 19th century, would find its earliest complete statement in the astounding late works of Monet. Clearly, Monet wished to immerse himself in his universe of light and water, with its fluid exits and entrances in our intermittent vision. There was always for Monet the graze of light that would emerge and disappear from one canvas to another. His "Nymphéas," so perfectly ensconced in the Orangerie, could easily be perceived in a different sequence and perhaps elsewhere, for their correspondences are interior. This occurs even in his more specific paintings, such as the rows of cypresses that fill up a space, then another and another space, but always a space that has ambiguous lineaments. Rothko may have thought of Monet. In Monet the idea of transcendence, with its complex paradoxes, is explicit: Monet sits in Giverny, waiting to entrap his moment. Monet works in a scale in which he must invoke time, and live time as he travels from side to side on his canvas. Monet gives himself to the water and tries, like an alchemist, to change the heaviness, the quantitativeness of pigment and its oil binder to the fluidity of air and water. Monet transcends his vision and creates a little universe of elements. Each day he begins again. Each day his painting ritual is to approach the same motif and to wring from it equivalents to his emotional furor. He too wished to dissolve himself, or his self, into a whole, a universe whose silence reverberates.

Despite the fiasco of the Seagram affair, Rothko was eager to find again an opportunity to create his own environment via painting in a public place; a possibility of "translating pictorial concepts into murals which would serve as an image for a public place." Since Rothko always chose his words carefully for publication, his diction here is important. He starts with pictorial concepts—individual paintings. They are to be translated into murals (his love for the prefix -*trans*). These murals are plural but they will serve as *an* image for a public place. In other words, the spectator will come away with an after-image that is whole, a harmonious whole that creates a unique atmosphere in the imagination, as would a symphony on the morrow of a memorable concert. Soon after Rothko completed the Seagram works, Wassily Leontief, a Nobel Prize winning economist who had admired Rothko and been a friend for some years, approached his colleagues of the Society of Fellows at Harvard University with a proposal that Rothko be commissioned to create murals for their future quarters. Most of the Fellows, as Leontief remembers with gentle amusement, were baffled by Rothko's work, but with a little persuasion succumbed to their chairman's enthusiasm. The murals were intended for the penthouse of the Holyoke Center designed by José Luis Sert. Rothko went through the ceremonious interview with Harvard's Fellows with considerable aplomb, and even his interview with Harvard's president did not unnerve him, much to Leontief's relief. Here too, however, there was to be a snag. Before Rothko's murals were installed, the Harvard Corporation decided to use the penthouse not for the Fellows, but for a dining room for official entertainment. Rothko's calm response to the preliminary maneuvers for his Harvard commission reflected his general attitude in the late 1950s and early 1960s. He was feeling far more confident and had experienced several moments of inner satisfaction, both in his works and in their reception. In 1959, for instance, he had been at the cocktail party offered by Monroe Wheeler in the Museum of Modern Art's guest house in honor of Miró. Rothko had approached Miró to say how much he owed to him, and Miró had turned, smiling, and replied, "And I owe a great deal to *you*, Mr. Rothko." Another event—the installation of his own room in the Phillips Collection in Washington—also brought Rothko satisfaction. Probably even the moment when he refused the Guggenheim International Award, writing James Johnson Sweeney that he looked forward to the time when "honors can be bestowed, simply, for the meaning of a man's life's work," also bolstered his self-esteem. Rothko began work on the Harvard cycle in 1961 and finished in 1962, bringing some of the pictorial concepts broached in the Seagram murals to fruition. He spoke, at the time of their installation, of the "oval" character of his enterprise (calling to mind the romantic Herder's allusion to the ellipse: our planet, Herder wrote, moves always around the two foci of our ellipse, knowing and feeling, and is seldom equally near each). In the Harvard cycle of five panels, Rothko's planet moves magnetically toward the pole of pure feeling, but there is a steady reference to knowing, or to a concept. His intention was to suffuse a given space with an atmosphere created entirely by the light and attendant shadows residing within his paintings. He could be in complete command of the emotional responses of his viewers because not only would he control the position of his paintings in relation to the space within which the viewers circulate, but he also controls the definition of the room. From any point in the room, which at Harvard was far from congenial to Rothko's purposes, the paintings surround and work on the sensibilities of its inhabitants. The room Rothko had to accommodate was awkward. Two of its walls were glazed so that the room itself became little more than a corridor between large horizontal windows. Details, such as heavy glass doors and clumsy louvers hiding air conditioning units were intrusive. Yet, they were canceled by the paintings, which managed to expand and engulf despite windows, doors, and heavy dining chairs that partially obstructed the canvases.

Rothko did his best to calculate the light in his "corridor" of paintings, knowing that time—one of the important ingredients in his work—would collaborate with him. These representations of sequences of feelings that have what Coleridge called "companionable form," as does the flame in the hearth, reveal themselves in time. The major triptych on the long wall tended to change character hour by hour. In the midday light the central horizontal canvas with its plum reds reading through blacks and its irregularities of form and value took on a silvery effulgence. The same three can-

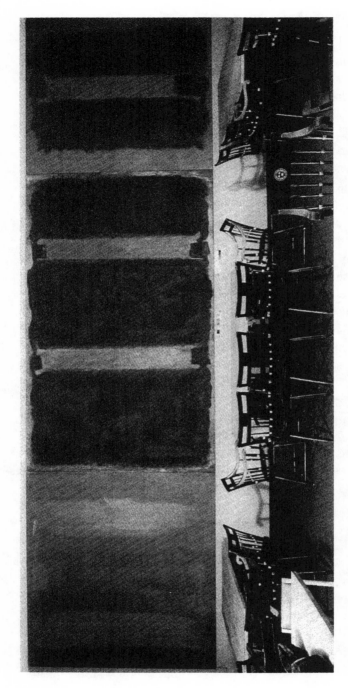

28. *Triptych*, Panels 1, 2, 3 of the Harvard Murals 1962

vases in the late afternoon became a densely textured, mysterious mass of cryptic shadows. To the right, the wine red forms of central verticals seem to curve inward, with depth given in the blue-gray tones that can be read below the surface. In the oblique light of waning day this panel with its central rectangular forms feathered on both inner and outer edges pulsates in long, slow rhythms. Contrasting with the langorous mystery of the darker panels is the leftward panel. Because of our reading habit, it is the first of the sequence, but could as well be the last. A fiery orange-red form is suspended like a flaming hoop in purple space, an apparition that appears in its own theater with its own transforming inner stage lights. It too is susceptible to time, and as it is contemplated, the low rectangular knot—the plaquette suspended on a horizontal line that is repeated top and bottom in each painting—becomes a glowing coal, with thicker brush marks and vermilion splashes like lambent sparks. In these paintings Rothko is concerned with conventional values of chiaroscuro posed in unconventional terms. Like many painters in history, he is deeply concerned with the almost indefinable areas between obscurity and light—a concern that would later become absolute. Depth is assured in various ways. There is never a single opaque surface, but a membranous, respiring foreplane image through which several levels of light and shadow announce themselves. Undercurrents are the very heart of Rothko's image. His depth expresses itself also in the way there is never a straight edge—the obvious means to assert frontality and hold to the plane. He takes care to make his roughly rectangular forms ambiguous, always tapering the edges and sometimes grading them off into four or five values so that, symbolically, the viewer can read far back. He used his brush to ensure such reading, as in a red and white, squarish panel in which the white has pink-to-gray intonations that constantly change. The brush established stages in a space that is, as always in Rothko, not exactly circumscribed, described, or bounded. Each painting in this mural cycle has a heart, and each has a pulse dictated by that hidden heart.

By the time Rothko had completed the Harvard murals, he had arrived at a position of considerable importance and was generally regarded as a master, even in the public press. Yet the meaning of his life's work had been rarely discussed in the art press. Rothko had no single powerful advocate, although several extremely sensitive appraisals had appeared during the 1950s. The earliest article dealing with the abstractions was by a West Coast painter, Hubert Crehan, who had acquired his interest during his days around the California School of Fine Arts. Crehan understood long before the others that Rothko was engaged in an undertaking that could find little expression in words. He wrote in 1954 of Rothko's "wall of light" and pointed out that "This rational attempt to destroy the line is undoubtedly based on Rothko's intuitions of the essential oneness of things—a kind of visual metaphor of the unity and integrity of life, consciousness and the universe."[72] In his enthusiasm, Crehan referred to Rothko as a prophet come down from the mountain—which was enough to set Rothko against his interpretation, jealous, as he always was, of his reputation as a "materialist." The next cogent interpretation of his work appeared only in 1957 when Elaine de Kooning wrote "It is no accident that a painting by Rothko is a façade, almost as though his art were trying to hide behind itself."[73] This response also met with Rothko's disfavor, despite his having "sat" for the article at de Kooning's studio, as she wryly reported. Rothko objected largely because de Kooning had lumped him together with others in the New York School. There were occasional sympathetic shorter reviews of his exhibitions during the 1950s, first at the Betty Parsons Gallery, where he showed almost yearly from 1949 to 1954, and then at the Sidney Janis, where he showed in 1955 and 1957. He had shifted to Janis because, as he told Betty Parsons, "I'm doing you no good and you're doing me no good." It was true enough that while Parsons went to great lengths to sell Rothko's works, even taking cuts in her own commissions, he was not flourishing. He had a reputation of distinction, though, and critics such as Thomas B. Hess were attentive whenever a work of his appeared. In 1955 (*Art News,* Summer) Hess observed that "Rothko approaches the classical, Renaissance problem of achieving the elemental serenity of symmetry in a way that avoids the paralyzing boredom perfect symmetry aspires to. Like Bramante or Piero della Francesca, he asks the riddle: 'What is living and stable?' and his answer is a balance of equalities disguised by scale."

162

The fact was that Rothko longed to be understood and he keenly missed searching commentary. As early as 1950 he had told Seitz that writing on art should never be comparative, historical, or analytical, but should record direct responses "in terms of human need." And to Katherine Kuh, he had written in 1954:

> If I must place my trust somewhere, I would invest it in the psyche of sensitive observers who are free of the conventions of understanding. I would have no apprehension about the use they would make of these pictures for the needs of their own spirits. For if there is both need and spirit there is bound to be a real transaction.[74]

Real transactions, Rothko felt, could not occur in conventional criticism, much as he craved understanding. It would not be until his one-man exhibition at the Museum of Modern Art in 1961 that the "meaning of a man's life work" would be pondered by many intelligent writers, and that Rothko could find a measure of satisfaction. The exhibition was organized by Peter Selz, whose enthusiasm made him a willing accomplice to Rothko's eccentric views about how his work should be presented, and what should be represented. Rothko decided to omit work before 1945, and to stress the work of the 1950s. He hung his paintings closely, and, attempting to fulfill the conditions of an intimacy, a space that takes the viewer into it, he worked with very low grade lighting, allowing the light of his canvases to breathe freely. During the exhibition Rothko visited the museum often. He had effectively moved into a new phase, and even his way of thinking about his work had altered. He told Selz, who quoted him in the catalogue, that as he had grown older Shakespeare had come closer to him than Aeschylus because "Shakespeare's tragic concept embodies for me the full range of life from which the artist draws all his tragic materials, including irony; irony becomes a weapon against fate." The injection of irony—a quality relatively absent from most American painting—was a defensive weapon for Rothko, whose general uneasiness in the world grew rapidly as his fame augmented. He was in his late fifties, and he knew that in spite of all the adulation, he would never become a patriarch. Already the "art world" was moving elsewhere, enshrining and thereby leaving behind the old master Abstract Expressionists.

Still, the exhibition drew an unprecedented response, and there were numerous reviews, some showing that their authors had undergone the experiences that Rothko thought could be available in his "tragic" works. Georgine Oeri, a European curator at the Guggenheim Museum, exceptionally sensitive, wrote an appreciation of the exhibition that eloquently spoke for those who were moved by Rothko's canvases. Oeri had been quietly appreciative for several years. With her there had been "a real transaction." She avoided the traps of history and analysis that Rothko so scorned. Her culture made it possible for her to understand what Rothko meant when he spoke of irony as "a sort of self-effacement, a self-examination in which a man can for a moment escape his fate," and when he insisted that an artist makes a decision about "the kind of civilization he tries to present," adding that he was interested only in *this* civilization. Oeri understood the edge on which Rothko balanced so precariously, writing that Rothko's audacity "is not unlike that of Moses who dared to say 'I will now turn aside, and see this great sight, why the bush is not burnt.'" She well understood Rothko's suspicion of critics, writing in her first paragraph of response to the Museum of Modern Art show:[75]

> The audacity of the inspired is never welcome; neither is their testimony. It implies demands upon the world which are resented or rejected all the more because the right or justification to make these demands can never be verified. That which is obvious is not revealing to everybody . . .

Oeri goes on to say that there are good reasons not to propel Rothko's work into "eschatalogical" dimensions, but states what she sees as Rothko's fundamental premise: the confidence in the naturalness of the spirit and in the possibility of its being manifest. She saw that the exhibition as a whole "evoked the sensation of a living organism. All of its parts shared the animation of being in and of the present, participated equally in the composition of a festive and grandly serious place." Like Willem de Kooning, whose response to the show was to speak of a house with many mansions, Oeri understood Rothko's preoccupation with reciprocal spaces and gave one of the best descriptions of how the show looked:

The exhibition galleries were interconnected in such a way that at various crossroads, one faced the huge expanses of the closely hung Rothko canvases, no matter which way one turned. The more they looked different, the more they looked the same and the more they looked the same, the more they looked different.

As Rothko moved from the late 1940s into the 1950s, Oeri remarked that the space "vacated by the early world of phenomena is filled with color which now becomes the evocative instrument," an instrument, she says, that is "impelled to transcend its pictorial quality, to become itself the transforming agent of the substance of which it is made, rendered permeable by the meaning it embodies." Oeri understood a drive in Rothko that would only later become apparent to others when she says of his color, "It is the substance by which that is substantiated which has no substance."

Oeri's opening with the Mosaic allusion would be enough to put Rothko off. Robert Goldwater, however, in his review of the exhibition, won his approval. Goldwater did not attempt to penetrate Rothko's "façade." Rothko was so pleased that he insisted that Goldwater's article be reprinted in the catalogues in Europe when his exhibition traveled in 1962. Goldwater opened his reflections on the exhibition with a bold insight:

> In Mark Rothko's picture the apparent end lies close to the apparent beginning—so close, in fact, or in apparent fact, that they are almost indistinguishable.[76]

He then follows with gratifying (to Rothko) obedience to Rothko's public statements, saying that "Rothko's concern over the years has been the reduction of his vehicle to the unique colored surface which represents nothing and suggests nothing else." Here, Goldwater no doubt missed Rothko's irony. "They say they are façades," he used to say with a malicious chuckle, "so they *are* façades." Goldwater shares Rothko's contempt for "literary fancies" and tries to persuade his readers to forget such "program notes" and to pay attention to the canvases themselves. Yet, to Rothko himself, his colored surfaces, although they "represented nothing" did, contrary to Goldwater's assertion, suggest something else. He never abandoned the will to portray. His paintings, he would maintain in pri-

29. Mark Rothko on his birthday in 1960

vate, were "portraits" of states of the soul, and inevitably were both objects in themselves, and something else. The element of allegory was never foreign to him.

When the British assessed the exhibition, they were rapt. Bryan Robertson, writing in the catalogue for the Whitechapel Gallery (Oct.-Nov. 1961), marveled at the body of work and its emotional power, concluding that "We are left with a presence rather than a specific identity." David Sylvester, writing in *The New Statesman* (Oct. 20, 1968), thought the paintings "the complete fulfillment of Van Gogh's notion of using color to convey man's passion," while Alan Bowness in *The Observer* (Oct. 15, 1961) thought that "Rothko plays Seurat to Pollock's Van Gogh." The painter-critic Andrew Forge was overwhelmed. "When I first saw Rothko's work I felt I had fallen into a dream,"[77] he said, adding that the imperative to go up close was compelling. As the show traveled, there were other strong responses, mostly of awe, and Rothko's reputation as a master was confirmed in capital after capital. And yet he was uneasy. He sometimes doubted greatly. He often fell into depression. He felt not at home in the world, and above all the art world that in the 1960s seemed so promiscuous, so superficial. By the mid-1960s, Philip Guston reported, "Rothko too thought that the smoke that existed ten years ago was a false situation; this is the *real* situation."[78] In this "real" situation of isolation, brought on by fame and the waning of New York School influence, Rothko continued to work for a time in the moody vein established in the two mural cycles but felt increasingly nervous about his direction. His craving to "control the situation" had grown more insistent, while "the situation" had become less and less clear.

10

The controversy over the real meaning of Rothko's work (metaphysical or physical?) would be rendered pointless when, in 1964, he eagerly seized the opportunity to create a Catholic chapel in Houston, Texas. Christian themes were not foreign to him. He had painted a Last Supper in his Greek manner in the late 1930s, and a Crucifixion and Gethsemane. In the past he had tended to treat Biblical themes as part of the great mythological reserve Frazer had provided. By 1964 he unequivocally saw "human need" in terms of spirit. All the questions hovering around the meaning of his work were to be definitively answered in this undertaking. He felt increasingly uneasy in the world of interpreted things. He had had many honors but they provided transient satisfactions. While he accepted certain homages—such as the invitation to John F. Kennedy's inauguration and a state dinner for artists a few months later—he felt increasingly isolated and held himself apart. Occasionally he would indicate his disaffection in spirited tirades against the art world, sometimes to people he did not know well. Or, he would pour out his disappointments, angrily denouncing insensitive critics. He objected to those who were busy tracking down his Surrealist sources, telling Andrew Forge in 1963 that he had never swallowed the vulgarities of psychoanalytic jargon, and that his painting was far removed from the precincts of the unconscious with its supposed archetypes. In addition, he was increasingly appalled by the cultural and political situation and, like many other artists, looked upon the pumped-up promotion campaigns now attending the arts as inimical to the purposes of art. So, when the de Menils, who had admired his Seagram murals during a studio visit in 1962, came later with their offer of an entire chapel, Rothko was keenly receptive. John and Dominique de Menil were sympathetic patrons. They had a long history of friendship with artists and an exceptionally fine collection of modern art. They had shown understanding when Rothko had tried to explain why he finally rejected the Seagram commission. The de Menils were willing to invest complete faith in whatever Rothko would do. Philip Johnson drew up the original floor plan as an octagonal shape. This "pleased Rothko who had a special liking for the Torcello baptistry and church," Mrs. de Menil wrote.[79] As soon as plans had been drawn Rothko set to work in his new carriage-house studio on East 69th street, constructing a full-scale model of a segment of the chapel, simulating as closely as possible the ultimate structure.

Rothko had been given the commission in the late spring of 1964. In the summer he had taken his family to a rented cottage in Amagansett, Long Island, overlooking Gardiner's Bay, where he mused on his project. The commission seemed to bring a great release. During a visit I saw Rothko on his porch watching tenderly as his baby son Christopher clapped his hands while Schubert's Trout Quintet filled the air. He spoke distractedly of small domestic things during a lunch of hamburgers. After, we walked on the beach, and he became unusually animated. He talked of the new studio and the commission. His idea was to "make East and West merge in an octagonal chapel." This was an old dream. He had often spoken of reading the Patristic writers during his youth—a part of his self-education of which he was proud, and which seemed very odd to his earlier acquaintances. But Rothko's attraction to Origen and the other early Christian writers was completely in keeping with his temperament. What he liked, he said, was the "ballet of their thoughts." He said that in them, everything "went toward ladders." It was not unlikely that he was attracted to the Patristic writers because they were in rebellion against fixed traditions, and particularly against the empty rhetoric they discerned in late Greek thought. The fathers of the church were careful to mention as often as possible (at least in one aspect of their works) their contempt for "style" and their belief in elementary simplicity. The early fathers of the church spoke in a period of transition in which individual views were still valid and the church was not yet rigidly institutionalized. It was, as Werner Jaeger sees it, a historical encounter between two worlds, the Greek and the early Christian.[80] The Greek influence is rendered in the conception of the universe as an organic being. All its aspects are functional, as in the human organism; all the parts "breathe together," as Clement of Alexandria wrote. Moreover, the early fathers carried a humanistic tradition from Greek culture, often using the word *morphosis,* meaning "the formation of man," and not the theological terminology that dominated later Christian thought.

Rothko's harking back to the Patristic thinkers was a necessary move for him. Every artist seeks or creates a tradition within which he can feel unique. Rothko had to invent a tradition, or a fiction of a tradition, because it is only in the contents of a life of the mind, that includes everyplace it has wandered, that an artist can find his style. Sometimes he must abandon his present in order to find it again and test it against the universal human table of contents he has carried for so many years. Rothko instinctively sought another context. He felt he was hemmed in by contemporary clichés. At times, he felt he had reached an impasse in his enterprise. Now he could set out again, gathering all he knew of human existence, in order to express its potential to transcend. He had traveled from self-expression to the grandly tragic as suggested by Nietzsche; from symbolism to silence; from Fra Angelico to the early Christians. Shuttling backward and forward in human history, spirituality was his goal.

In the "ballet" of the thoughts of the Greek fathers of the church, there were many endearing allusions to the visible beauties of life in the world; many simple descriptions of life in monastic retreats. There was even jesting and teasing in letters exchanged. The view of the world expressed by Origen and generally held by the early fathers was that of a whole organism, "some huge and immense animal which is held together by the power and reason of God as by

170

one soul." Creation, according to Gregory of Nazianzus, is "a system and compound of earth and sky and all that is in them, an admirable creation indeed when we look at the beautiful form of every part, but yet more worthy of admiration when we consider the harmony and unison of the whole, and how each part fits with every other in fair order, and all with the whole, tending to the perfect completion of the world as a unit."[81] Reading such passages, Rothko primed himself for his task. In Gregory of Nyssa, Rothko could warm to the dream of many artists, symbolized in the ladder, known so well through the terse, mysterious passage in the Old Testament where Jacob lies dreaming. Ladders, wherever they appear in art, are instinct with symbolism that soars to spiritual realms. Gregory of Nyssa wrote that the man of half-formed intelligence, when he observes an object bathed in the glow of apparent beauty, thinks that the object in its essence is beautiful and goes no deeper. A more developed mind will see outward beauty as the ladder by which he climbs to that intellectual beauty from which all other beauties derive their existence, and their names, in proportion to their share in it.

Perhaps it was Origen's tendency to allegory, and his method of threefold interpretation that attracted Rothko. Origen described the three approaches to the scriptures as literal, ethical, and allegorical or, literal, historical, and spiritual, in another translation. Rothko had had his literal phase; had been preoccupied with ethical interpretations; and would, finally, arrive at the ultimate spiritual allegory in the chapel. The whole period in which the Greek theologians put forward their views attracted Rothko. Instinctively he was drawn to the cryptic, the hermetic. He liked the old baptistry in Torcello and Byzantine structures in general. In them, there is nothing "outer." The outer walls of Byzantine chapels are blank and impenetrable. Unadorned, they are merely the keepers of the treasure within. Rothko had seen Ravenna. The little cruciform chapel of Galla Placidia, with its nocturnal light created entirely within the tesserae crowning its dome, and its tiny windows of alabaster, lingered perhaps in his memory, for there are few monuments in history with a space as complete and as controlled by the artist whose signature is in the unique light he has produced. An inscription in

the archiepiscopal chapel in Ravenna (certainly it would be a dis-
covery of moment for Rothko) reads: "The light is either born here
or, imprisoned, reigns here in freedom" (*Aut lux nata aut capta hic
libera regnat*). The central apse in the basilica in Torcello also stim-
ulated Rothko's vision of spiritual light. There is a rare apparition
of an elongated madonna and child, standing on a symbolic, dis-
embodied small rectangular platform against a vast absence created
in gold. The totally abstract gold ground of the curving wall of the
apse gives an immense sense of transcendence. For the worshipers
of the late antique period, the churches were *ho topos*, "the place"
in which, as Peter R. L. Brown has written, "it was possible to share
for a moment in the eternal repose of the saints in paradise. Light
seems trapped in the churches. The blaze of lamps and gold mosaic
recapture the first moment of Creation: 'Dark chaos is fled away.' "[82]
For Rothko, *ho topos* had been an obsession for many years, and the
flight from dark chaos an ideal of long standing. As he worked he
seemed intent on making "the place" where, in its grand abstract
realm, necessity is fled along with chaos.

When Rothko returned from Long Island in the fall of 1964 he
began working in earnest. The huge studio with its central skylight
shielded by parachute silk became a place as he imagined it, differ-
ent day after day, and re-made each day. As in his old gymnasium,
there was little to distract him. A bed, a couple of canvas captain's
chairs and hi-fi equipment were the only amenities visible. A series
of young assistants came to help him build the huge stretchers
which in themselves, even before they carried their canvas surfaces,
were of crucial importance to Rothko's imagined "jointed scheme."
There were times when Rothko sat for hours in his canvas chair,
contemplating the shape and size of the empty stretchers. His as-
sistants would be called upon to change one or another as Rothko
sought the absolute solution to his fourteen-sided scheme. Eventu-
ally the job of stretching the canvas replaced that of contemplating.
That would take nearly a month, so careful was he that surfaces be
exactly even and permanently stretched. Then Rothko would begin
his painstaking procedure of preparing the ground—a procedure
recommended by the old masters in which he boiled rabbit's glue
and mixed dry pigment together with oil and a little turpentine.
These grounds, composed very largely of Alizarin crimson and

black, were laid on swiftly by his assistants, and had to be smooth but not monotonous—a job that kept his assistants sweating. In these decisions Rothko was slow but assured. Once the canvases had their "plum" grounds, they would be aligned in the replica of the chapel and Rothko would again sit and contemplate them. Finally, as Roy Edwards, one of his assistants recounts, he would decide where to place a black rectangle and the assistant would dust it in with charcoal.[83] These interior shapes were then contemplated for days, singly and in relation to others. Rothko would sometimes decide to change the distance of the dominant shape from the border by a quarter of an inch, or, if he had already painted the dark interior, he would put the canvas away and substitute another. Months went by with this elaborate procedure, with Rothko inching toward his vision.

Rothko's choice of two basic colors—black and red—and their light-reflecting variants helped to define his image (for it was to be a single image finally). The degrees of light available in these color juxtapositions were calculated broadly, for it was an *effect* he sought and not a mechanical scheme. He was enough of a Nietzschean to be wary of systems. Nietzsche had nothing but contempt for systems that were airtight, writing,

> The will to a system: in a philosophy, morally speaking, a subtle corruption, a disease of the character; amorally speaking, his will to pose as more stupid than he is, more stupid, that means: stronger, simpler, more commanding, less educated, more masterful, more tyrannical.

Rothko had come to think of his chapel as a matter of finding the right proportions in an almost mystical way, like the alchemist. Proportion with its manifold implications: the right proportion, as the Greeks had suggested to him in his youth, tempers a man's life; the right proportion of pigment to oil brings him his light; the right proportion of thing to infinite space defines a man's stance in a world only he can construe. Morton Feldman understood as a fellow artist can understand when, of all his recollections of encounters with Rothko, he chose to talk about a visit to the Metropolitan Museum in which Rothko made his way to a small room of Greco-Roman sculpture:

Rothko always followed through his reaction to something that would catch his attention with a brief, reflective commentary. I remember his absorption one afternoon with the Greco-Roman sculpture: "How simple it would be if we all used the same dimension—the way these sculptures here resemble each other in height, stance, and the distance between one foot and the other."

Feldman's comment is astute: "Rothko was leaning toward a possible *answer* in a more subliminal mathematics of his own work."[84] Such "subliminal mathematics" has to do with one of the most perplexing and mysterious problems in the visual arts—the problem of scale. Every art student knows that scale is not the same as size. And most art students have been accustomed to thinking about scale as a problem of relative proportions. But Rothko, and some of his colleagues in the New York School had had a glimpse of another way of creating scale—a dazzling vision that not even the most intelligent among the painters could quite pin down. He envisioned his task in the chapel as a clarification of this eternal painterly problem. He would, with the right proportions of color and shape, substantiate, as Oeri wrote, that which has no substance.

There were often visitors to the studio and Rothko would sit, contemplating his work in progress, awaiting responses, although no one could gauge how much he was dependent on response. When old painting friends such as de Kooning or Motherwell or Guston visited, there was talk about "the situation," and sometimes about the murals. Motherwell visited early in 1967 and came away with a profound respect. "They are truly religious," he commented, adding that Rothko had said that he had become "a master of proportion." Motherwell quoted Rothko as saying that in the beginning he had thought of them as pictures. But then, he considered that people praying would not want to be distracted by pictures. They wanted an ambiance.[85] Of course an ambiance is what Rothko wanted, composed of rhythm, proportion, and transcending emotion—rhythm in the sense that Hölderlin sang of it,

> All is rhythm; the entire destiny of man is a single
> celestial rhythm, just as the work of art
> is a unique rhythm.

Rothko, when he made the decision to leave certain of his murals bereft of image was certainly thinking of a unique rhythm. He was shaping the "absent," as Mallarmé was shaping it in his singular final work "Un Coup de dés." Like Mallarmé he had gone from a technique of metamorphosis to something nearer in meaning, to transfiguration. Proportions seemed to be the key. In the context of Rothko's last works, it is possible to understand what he admired in Mondrian (for he *did* admire Mondrian, and was proud when Mondrian's disciple Fritz Glarner told him that he was closer to Mondrian than anyone else. He even lectured on "the sensuousness of Mondrian").

Rothko had said that a painter's work would move toward clarity. When in January 1965 he wrote a careful memorial speech for his old friend Milton Avery—a speech for which there were several well-worked drafts—he was himself at work on the Houston murals. His thoughts turned to Avery's walls "covered with an endless and changing array of poetry and light." Avery, he said, "had that inner power in which gentleness and silence proved more audible and poignant." Most important, Avery had nothing "tentative" about him, he had "naturalness," "exactness," and the "inevitable completeness" that Rothko posited as the highest values. Such thoughts had no locus in the contemporary art world from which Rothko felt so alienated. Rather, he would have had to turn back to find another climate of thought. Like Stephen Dedalus, he found himself in another era in which the question of *claritas* seemed urgent. Joyce's need to discuss the old scholastic notions of aesthetics sprang from a similar disaffection with the art of his time; the same need to find a new approach by rejecting the clamor of the day's encounters. In "Portrait of the Artist" Stephen wanders about the streets of Dublin discoursing on the Thomist aesthetic, trying to find his way among the three things Aquinas has said are essential to beauty: wholeness, or *integritas;* harmony, or *consonantia*, and radiance, or *claritas*. Radiance Joyce decided was equivalent to the scholastic notion of *quidditas*, or the *whatness* of a thing, without which a work of art cannot be realized. Joyce considered the highest form of art to be dramatic, and even in this early work, envisioned his life's task. The dramatic form is reached, he said,

> when vitality which has flowed and eddied round each person fills every person with such vital force that he or she assumes a proper and intangible esthetic life. . . . The esthetic image in

the dramatic form is life purified in and reprojected from the human imagination. . . . The artist, like the God of creation, remains within or behind or beyond or above his handiwork, invisible, refined out of existence, indifferent, paring his fingernails . . .

This medieval frame for his thoughts suited Joyce's instincts as an artist, and were equally suitable to Rothko's final enterprise. His monastic intentions are undeniable in this last expression of universal silence—intentions as ascetic as Fra Angelico's in the late works for his monastic brothers. This final work would be "the place" where the artist, as Rothko had said a few years earlier, would surpass his "self." He took his task absolutely seriously, as his letter to John de Menil (Jan. 1, 1966) suggests:

The magnitude on every level of experience and meaning, of the task in which you have involved me exceeds all my preconceptions. And it is teaching me to extend myself beyond what I thought was possible for me. For this I thank you.

The will to sink into a whole, the dissolution into a universe that, as Nietzsche and then Joyce had imagined, would absorb the individuality of the artist, had always been latent in Rothko. Wells, caves, retreats are implicit in the depths of certain of his works where the light has been dimmed almost to extinction. Why had he painstakingly developed a technique of overlaying colors until his surfaces were velvety as poems of the night? Sometimes in his works of the late 1950s he would allow hints of striations in the middle sections of his paintings—bars of indeterminate color that suggest the river flow, eternal flux. The elements had breathed in his works, and for the chapel, he would still maintain their pulsation under the final surfaces of his panels. Light was meant to flow from one to the other, unimpeded by detail. The scheme for the chapel would fulfill his vision, expressed some fifteen years earlier, when he told Seitz that antitheses are neither synthesized nor neutralized in his work but held in a confronted unity which is a momentary stasis.

Such stasis is not foreign to the religious experience. The question has often been raised: was Rothko religious? I don't think he was religious in any conventional sense. More likely he was religious in the way Matisse was religious when he undertook the Vence chapel. Matisse said, after its completion, in his letter to Bishop Rémond that this work represented the result of his entire life and that it issued from a life consecrated to the search for truth. In his notes for the chapel booklet, he said that the chapel had afforded him the possibility of realizing all his life's researches "by uniting them," and that the chapel was the flower of an "enormous, sincere and difficult effort."[86] To the degree that the magnitude of Rothko's task on every level exceeded all his preconceptions, as Rothko wrote, he put himself in what might be called a psychological condition of religiousness. This was not as difficult for him as might be thought. This Russian, who had consumed his Dostoyevsky and had always charged himself with ethical conundrums, could imagine a place in which there could be solace for the secular. His chapel would not be an experience of private meditation such as those who contemplate mandalas undergo, but an experience of the summum of a spiritual man's life's work, where all his researches, in Matisse's terms, could be united. The expression of faith had to be a faith in the Existentialist idea of intersubjectivity—the only faith left to modern man. The highest praise in Rothko's vocabulary, as Motherwell remarked, was to call someone a "human being," that is, a person who feels.

Yet, Rothko was a Jew, had learned to pray in Hebrew, and known the humiliations of Jewishness. He always said he would never have worked for a synagogue. He did not explain, but one could speculate that for him, the chapel was already a distancing, an opportunity to stand back and generalize his deepest feeling about existence. He could not have stepped back in a synagogue in which so many conflicting emotions resided for the modern Jew. He did think of himself as a Jew, as is apparent in a dramatic encounter ingenuously described by the German art historian Werner Haftmann. Haftmann visited Rothko in 1959 to ask him to participate in "Documenta," the large international exhibition. Rothko refused saying that "as a Jew, he had no intention of exhibiting his works in Germany, a country that had committed so many crimes against Jewry."[87] After further conversation, Haftmann reported, Rothko looked at him squarely and said that if he "could manage to have even a very small chapel of expiation erected in memory of Jewish victims, he would paint this without any fee—even in Germany, which he hated so much. He then said it need only be a tent." This passionate expression of Rothko's deep personal response to the Holocaust led Haftmann to fanciful conclusions concerning the nature of Rothko's enterprise that, had Rothko lived to read them, would probably have appalled him. Haftmann seized upon the "tent" allusion and wove a fantasy in which the "swaying" quality he detected in certain of Rothko's largest pictures took on the character of curtains which in turn evoked old Jewish metaphors of the temple curtains in front of the Holy of Holies. This led Haftmann to assume that the source of all of Rothko's work lay in his "Eastern Jewish humanity" and that Jewry, which remained amorphous for more than two thousand years, had found its own pictorial expression.

This interpretation denies one of Rothko's most impelling arguments: that he was a 20th-century man nurtured on Nietzsche and well aware of the futility of ancient gestures. Like the young Malevich, whose spirit his most nearly resembles, Rothko sought a godless expression of godliness. He too had emotional responses that, as Malevich said, led to the desert of pure feeling. The kind of universe Malevich had in mind was boundless, yet encompassable or "felt" by the imagination which could intuit its very boundlessness. Malevich built for himself an objectless world. Swept clean of centuries of painterly clutter, Malevich's world, expressed for him first in a black square on a white ground, was secure from the ravages of daily life. It was "elsewhere." The diction of his manifestos indicates his fervent will to translate himself into another climate—one of great clear spaces and pure light. His written language is ecstatic, and he envisioned a plastic language equal to his visions. This plastic language of "weights" and "movements," rather than forms and colors, was posited to be read by kindred spirits in whom Malevich had confidence. Eventually his project was confirmed: generations of artists were at home with this objectless language of pure feeling. It became one of the available idioms for Rothko's generation. Not only could they wield its philosophical principles, but they could, as did Rothko, see Byzantine and Trecento art through its lens. If

Rothko insisted that he was a "materialist" and a 20th-century man, he meant that he was forsaken in the world, as all humans are, just as Nietzsche said man would be forsaken until, by his own will, he would become an overman, in control of his personal destiny. The thoughts of a man of the cloth, Father Couturier, who had engaged many modern artists in church decoration, are closer to Rothko's situation than those of the art historian: Father Couturier thought that "Genius doesn't give faith, but there is between mystical inspiration and that of heroes and great artists a profound analogy."

As Rothko sat in his captain's chair, contemplating his masterwork month after month, he had diverse thoughts, some of which he voiced to friends. Early in 1966 he looked at one of his mural sequences and said, "I'm only interested in precision now." He stressed his new quest for proportion when he said "even when I used to use three colors, say purple, yellow and red, if I saw them in relativity, I had to do something else." In the fall, after he had returned from an important sojourn in Europe, he mused, "You never know where your work will take you," adding that in the Houston cycle he was interested neither in symmetry or asymmetry, but only in proportions and shapes. In early spring of 1967, when a mysterious melancholy had overtaken him, Rothko was contemplating one of the triptychs—the center panel an obscure color of red-brown-gray mixture, with oxblood borders; the two side panels uniform oxblood— and remarked, "I wanted to paint both the finite and the infinite." This reminded him of the work of Ad Reinhardt, who had resolutely eliminated both color and individual form from his recent work. "The difference between me and Reinhardt is that he's a mystic. By that I mean that his paintings are immaterial. Mine are *here*. Materially. The surfaces, the work of the brush and so on. His are untouchable." His thoughts then shifted to the morning's crisis in Israel, the so-called war of attrition, and he asked, as he often asked in his last years, "Will the world last another decade?"[88] The somberness that most people felt in the studio; the feeling of solitariness; the kind of hushed space in which Rothko worked in his last years made for an atmosphere that could be perceived as sacred, or at least, associated with the interiors of sacred places such as Byzantine churches. However, Rothko's vision, at least in its

30. In Rome, 1966: Rothko, the painter Carlo Battaglia,
Rothko's son Christopher, and his wife Mell

religious dimension, if there were one, was not bounded by his early Jewish formation, or by his admiration for any other culture, or by any special feeling for Catholicism. If anything, the light in the Houston murals called to mind Pascal's "Deus absconditus," a far more troubled and modern conception of the fled deity.

As Rothko carried his work along from month to month and year to year, he struggled to refine his conception, and his mood darkened. In a kind of aesthetic despair (whose sources he had long ago examined in the light of Kierkegaard) he worked out many schema in which differences became increasingly minute. By the spring of 1966 he felt he had settled on a satisfactory but perhaps not final scheme and decided to take a break by making a journey to Europe. Once there his depression lifted, and, especially in Rome, he set out to re-examine places that had moved him on his previous trips. Comfortably settled in the Battaglias' spacious apartment in the Palazzo Cenci, Rothko spent hours lounging on the leather couch, listening to *The Magic Flute* and *The Abduction from the Seraglio*, abstracted, removed, perhaps reviewing his project. At times he would stand at the window overlooking the piazza below in which a fountain played softly, singing to himself. In late afternoon he saw swallows swiftly descending to the basin of the fountain. He found a kind of peace in Rome that was to be later translated in the Houston chapel.

He also found warm responses and good conversation, and, as was often the case with Rothko, he revealed himself more fully to those with whom he had not had long and close relationships. In Rome he revisited Argan, where he discussed Fra Angelico again, and he spent time with the Scialojas. With Carlo Battaglia, he visited the oldest churches in Rome, peering closely at mosaics and frescoes from the earliest Christian period. They made a trip to Arezzo as well, where Rothko was dismayed. The Pieros were too much like illustrations he said, comic strips even. He did not like the Cinquencento and preferred the more conceptual mysteries of the early Renaissance. He tended to look at painting as a message, Toti Scialoja noted, recalling a visit to his own studio where Rothko looked seriously at one of Scialoja's abstractions with vertical forms and finally said, "I can understand that two are man and woman, three are man, woman and child, but five are nothing." Rothko could not like Piero, Scialoja felt, because Rothko "voyait avec des yeux symboliques."

From Rome the Rothko family traveled to France, Belgium, and Holland, concluding their journey in England. England had long been a beacon for Rothko, who had found a specially cordial reception during his first visit in the 1950s. The British painters had responded with exceptional fervor to their first exposure to his work in 1956 when the traveling exhibition *Modern Art in the U.S.A.* was shown in London. On each subsequent occasion when Rothko's work appeared in London (in the *The New American Painting* at the Tate in 1959, and in his one-man exhibition at the Whitechapel in 1961) enthusiasm mounted. Critics in Britain were generally reverent and often wrote lengthy articles that must have gratified Rothko, who always felt the critics in the United States were short of breath. The adulation of younger painters and their unreserved praise warmed him. A glimpse of what Rothko meant to that first postwar generation is caught in a letter to the *Times* of London written by William Scott and Paul Feiler after Rothko's death. They spoke of "his great human qualities" and pointed out that "when his work first appeared in England there was an immediate response on the part of a number of younger generation painters who recognized that here was a vital contribution made to the heritage of European landscape tradition through colour and light." They commented on his love for the English countryside and observed that "his knowledge of English literature was remarkable." They concluded, "Perhaps much of what happens today stems from that aesthetic shot which Mark Rothko gave us in 1956."

Rothko found satisfaction in the unreserved admiration tendered him during the course of the exhibition at the Whitechapel Gallery. The director of the gallery, Bryan Robertson, was sensitive to Rothko's needs, and had a strong feeling for the work. He made sure to report to Rothko that Henry Moore had made a special journey to London to see the show; had visited many times alone, and had said that Rothko's paintings were "his most revelatory experience in modern painting since his youthful discovery of Cézanne, Picasso, Matisse and the Cubists." Robertson added that the same was true of Sir Kenneth Clark and many others. "Rothko really loved England, and his affection for us and our foibles was so candid and unaffected that it took some time to realize that he was not joking, for even the inconveniences of English life for Rothko had a certain charm."[89] During his last visit Rothko conferred with Sir Norman Reid, the director of the Tate, and Andrew Forge, a trustee, over a long lunch, discussing the eventual Rothko room. Forge remembers Rothko's excited diatribe against Piero della Francesca, which led into a long speech against the idea of figuration in painting. "He spoke with a real sort of iconoclastic anger," Forge recalls. Both Reid and Forge sensed an uneasiness, probably related to Rothko's feeling that the world had turned to other things (things such as figurative art in its pop version, for instance). Reid mentions that Rothko asked again and again if he thought the young painters would be interested in the projected Rothko room, and Forge sensed that Rothko felt that he was, to the younger British connoisseurs, passé (which, as Forge points out, was probably true. By that time England had had major exhibitions of work by Robert Rauschenberg, Jasper Johns, and others in the new vanguard). To counteract Rothko's depression, Forge and the critic David Sylvester organized an evening with British artists who in fact admired Rothko greatly. But Rothko was not to be easily consoled.

When Rothko returned to his studio he had clarified his conception still further and set about making adjustments. His conflict with Philip Johnson over the eventual lighting of the chapel worried him. Rothko rejected Johnson's idea of a truncated pyramid that would allow light to diffuse the walls evenly, preferring to reproduce in Houston the skylight of his own studio. Mrs. de Menil recalled that "his love for familiar surroundings was such that he wanted also to have the same cement floor, and the same kind of walls . . . He liked irregularities, accidents. He liked ancient buildings with odd shapes, grown from 'the weaknesses and follies of men.' "[90] The conflict was only resolved when Johnson withdrew and the architects Howard Barnstone and Eugene Aubry took over, visiting Rothko and attending to his desires. (Johnson maintained later—and he was probably right—that Rothko had made a mistake about the lighting.)

The final scheme was to be fourteen canvases distributed symmetrically. In Mrs. de Menil's description:

> In the apse; a triptych of monochrome paintings fifteen feet high. To the right and left: two triptychs eleven feet high which had black fields. All the other paintings are again fifteen feet high. The four paintings on the four small sides of the octagon are monochromes, and almost eleven feet wide. The one at the entrance, only nine feet wide has again a black field.

In the actual chapel, when the paintings were installed after his death, the effects were disappointing. Rothko had been right to cherish "the place" that he had made in his own studio. The new place, with its concrete and steel, was, despite best intentions, far too perfect to be perfect for Rothko's vision. The problem of the searing Texas light could not be solved and it was only at certain moments late in the day that the chapel took on a semblance of the sacred aura so many had felt in Rothko's own studio. All the same, countless visitors to the Texas chapel (which had eventually been transformed into an ecumenical rather than Catholic chapel) experienced a kind of secular solace. Stanley Kunitz recalls a whole history of feelings. First, almost depression—they seemed to have such a bleakness of tonality. Later he grew to see the paintings in the changing light where he caught the sense of tranquility, and saw "all kinds of fluctuations." When he read his own poems in the chapel, finally, he was immensely moved.[91] This slow discovery by a poet is probably the best tribute to Rothko's enterprise. Another response by the art historian Robert Rosenblum stresses that the paintings evoke a traditional religious format:

> On three of the chapel's eight walls—the central, apse-like wall and the facing side walls—Rothko provided variations on the triptych shape, with the central panel alternately raised or level with the side panels. Yet these triptychs, in turn, are set into opposition with single panels, which are first seen as occupying a lesser role in the four angle walls but which then rise to the major role of finality and resolution in the fifth single panel which, different in color, tone and proportions, occupies the entrance wall, facing, as if in response, the triptych in the apse. It is as if the entire current of Western religious art were finally devoid of its narrative complexities and corporeal imagery, leav-

ing us with the dark, compelling presences that pose an ultimate choice between everything and nothing . . . the very lack of overt religious content here may make Rothko's surrogate icons and altarpieces, experienced in a nondenominational chapel, all the more potent in their evocation of the transcendental . . .[92]

Not all responses were equally sympathetic. Brian O'Doherty, who had harbored feelings of distaste for Rothko's occasional "schmaltzy sentimentality," questioned Rothko's position, reporting that Rothko had boasted that he could have fulfilled the commission with blank canvases "and made it work." Rothko's acute anxiety, O'Doherty declared, was "based on a suspicion that his most unsympathetic viewers shared—was there anything there at all?"[93] Such skepticism certainly lingered in the minds of many whose expectations were challenged by the final austerity of Rothko's scheme. Those who could believe were those who had a touch of the same aspiration, such as the composer Morton Feldman, who has described his music as "between Time and Space," saying that his compositions are not really compositions:" "One might call them time canvases in which I more or less prime the canvas with an overall hue of music." Commissioned in 1971 by the Menil Foundation to write a work in memory of Rothko, Feldman composed *The Rothko Chapel*. In his program notes, Feldman wrote:

> Like the chapel, the music is conceived in an ecumenical spirit. I think of it as a 'secular service.' I tried to create a music that walks the thin line between the abstraction of all art and the emotional longing that characterizes what it is to be 'human.' The chorus symbolizes art's abstractness; the solo viola, the need for human expression. It is only at the end of the work that I think of Rothko and his own love for melody. Here, I collage a Hebrewesque melody which I wrote thirty years ago—at sixteen.[94]

11

In 1958 Rothko had listed as one of the ingredients of a work of art the presence of irony—the "modern" ingredient. Greek tragedy didn't need it he said, but Shakespeare did. By his definition—that irony is a form of self-effacement and self-examination in which a man can for a moment escape his fate—the works of his last years permitted him few moments of escape. He was a natural heritor of a modern grief initiated long before, when doubt assailed the searchers. Pascal's *deus absconditus* was not the same God hidden in the Old Testament who was nonetheless there. Pascal's God eluded him endlessly. Faith would become a negative necessity, like, perhaps, space. The pain of the absence of faith and the great reservoir of doubt became the leitmotifs of the great minds of the 19th century.

Many modern artists had experienced a similar chill when confronting the Nothingness that had first become a motif in the 19th century. The situation of the modern artist was precisely that he was invested with the power to illuminate and inspire, but could not, as artists had before, assume the presence of a prime mover. Rothko was an Existentialist, finally, because he felt he had been as Heidegger said, "thrown into the world" and each time he had moments of ekstasis, he was thrust back into the human condition. O'Doherty was perhaps right when he suggested that Rothko doubted. But it was a high order of doubt. It had to do with the problem of possession: few modern painters can sustain the feeling that they have truly possessed their work, or experience. For Rothko and so many others, it was a matter of trying again, each time as anxiously as the last—anxious about what might be, what could be revealed. Rothko had maintained that the human enterprise in art would be to deal with the great themes of birth, dissolution, and death. "Tragic art, romantic art deals with the fact that a man is born to die."

The tranquil melancholy that prevails in the Houston chapel had not come upon Rothko suddenly. For a long time he had been a sad man. Even when he had achieved international renown on an unprecedented scale and could buy a large town house in an elegant neighborhood, he was perceived by friends as a man subject to serious depression. The quality of Rothko's sadness was understood by the Italian writer Gabriella Drudi, who visited New York in 1960 just after Rothko had acquired the grand house on East 95th Street:

> We went together to visit the house. There was happiness. The festiveness of the poor when they finally know possession. We climbed to the third floor where the studio would be; then to Tofy's room, and ended up sitting in the little courtyard—a bit melancholy as is every place that has been taken over by new inhabitants, still intruders. Mark had become taciturn and grim— this happened, I think, each time that he felt drawn into existence and not art. He seemed very tired. He said to Mell: you remember when I used to pass my days at the Museum of Modern Art looking at Matisse's *Red Studio?* You asked: why always that and only that picture? You thought I was wasting my time. But this house you owe to Matisse's *Red Studio*. And from those months and that looking every day all of my painting was born.[95]

Drudi observes that Rothko had said it not with the pride of one who had known how to "see" where he looked, nor with the firmness of one who tells about himself: "It was more the sad accent of the memory of a love; of the birth of a love." The sadness, the nostalgia for the birth of a love, dominated Rothko's last years. After the chapel paintings had been completed, Rothko was left with a great void. He had difficulties returning to the single easel painting. He felt displaced. Gradually he found a way again and produced several large and magnificent "afterstorms," as Rilke might have said. His working rhythm finally restored, Rothko was in somewhat better spirits when suddenly, in April 1968, he was struck down by a serious aneurysm. The gravity of the attack did not escape Rothko, whose brooding on death was habitual anyway. When he recovered enough to go with his family to Provincetown, he was in a black mood. All the same, he began a new series of works on paper, dark foreboding works of a sinking heart; blacks over purples and blacks over browns with an unaccustomed decisive line separating two rectangular areas in which, as he said, "the dark is always at the top." He himself was startled by these works and asked if it were agony or persuasiveness they represented. "All the crosses we load on our own shoulders," he wryly remarked in the fall of 1968, "when the world settles for things *without* crosses."[96] He felt increasingly remote from the preoccupations of the art world and from artists of the new generations. "We live at a point when the foremen are making the patterns," he commented, and then harked back to his incessant question: will the world last another decade?

Many old questions troubled him. In February 1969, I visited the studio. Highly nervous, thin, restless, Rothko chainsmoked and talked intermittently. Literature and music, he said, were his base. He was never really "connected" with painting, as he started painting only late. His material is his "inner life," his "inner experience." He has nothing to do with painting today, but rather is a Renaissance painter. (I was reminded that in the 1958 lecture he had firmly declared that in the great artistic epochs "Men with their minds produced a view of a world, transforming our vision of things.") With their minds . . . This was Rothko's vision of the Renaissance artist; his ideal which, in his isolation after his brush with death, he felt had been abandoned by all the world. The brooding and often harsh character of the many large paintings on paper he showed me that day could only be seen in the light of a man's sinking heart. The dark, he had said with unintentional symbolism, is always at the top. To Stamos, Morton Levine, Bernard Reis, and a few other close friends, he sometimes spoke of his aesthetic despair and the hollowness of his fame. He was convinced that on the whole he had never been properly understood.

There were many paintings from the last two years of Rothko's life. Some reverted to his older vision, but most were, he felt, new departures for perhaps another destination (although in the end Matisse was right, the destination is always the same). In some, he initiated the glaring white border, the blankness severely emphasized by the perfectly trued angles—with none of the "weaknesses and follies of men" at the outer limits. Only cold white light. The interiors were loosely painted: an area of dark above, a very fine line of light, and the fogged white-grays inflected at times with pinkish or bluish or ocherish hues below. Sometimes, during these last years, there were paintings in oil, and in them, Rothko occasionally used only gradations of black invoking his magical sheens. Like his cherished Fra Angelico, Rothko at the end of his life had no need of a range of colors. There was only one kind of light. The paintings with the brownish-grayish tonalities, done mostly in the winter of 1969, may well have been related to an event that had temporarily lightened Rothko's mood. In the winter of 1969, UNESCO headquarters in Paris had approached him about "doing" a room which would also have sculptures by Giacometti: He had long respected Giacometti whose work he saw as "tragic" in the lofty sense with which he always endowed that word. The thought of inhabiting, with his canvases, the same space as Giacometti's sculptures, was behind the series of brown-above-gray paintings on paper (meant to be mounted on canvas and stretchers). As Motherwell remarks, the colors were "not unlike the colors Giacometti himself used in his own figure paintings." In his conversation with Motherwell, Rothko referred to his new group of paintings as "a different world from myself"—one in which, as several other friends point out, he was not quite at ease.[97] Michel Butor wrote of earlier dark works, ". . . one of the most remarkable of Rothko's triumphs is to have made a kind of black light *shine*."[98] Now, the shine of black light and the shine of substantiated white light would be equivalent in these enigmatic last paintings. Butor refers to the conventional three areas in many of Rothko's earlier paintings as rungs of a Jacob's ladder. This Jacob's ladder was never literal, as the ladder of Jacob himself was not. The movement of the last paintings is equivocal. The resolute horizontality, stopped only by the white bands at the edges, seemingly denies an upward progression. The weighted darks at the summit are invested with deepening emotion. Long before, the French commentators had determined that, despite Rothko's disclaimers, his work was the work of a mystic. Philippe Sollers had written that "Rothko's interiorized, fiery furnace; his patently sacred enclosure where everything indicates a spiritual ambition . . . are opposed to the profane and radically rational space of Mondrian."[99] The painter Stamos was sensitive to the implicit tragedy in these last works and saw them as Goyesque.

Robert Goldwater, who had been authorized by Rothko to write a serious study of his life's work, edged closer to the kind of romantic reading he had once forsworn. Goldwater had spent time with Rothko during the difficult last period and reported that Rothko knew his last paintings were unlike anything he had ever done. But Rothko was guarded even with Goldwater: "In his comments, fragmentary, brief, punctuated with long and heavy silences, and in his questions, freighted with suppressed intensity, meanings were never mentioned."[100] Goldwater traced Rothko's descent to the lower register of color and to the solemn darkness of the last mural cycle, concluding that "the sense of the tragic" becomes increasingly dominant. The landscape implications of the stressed horizon line, according to Goldwater, were accepted by Rothko who was aware of the suggestion of deep space. Yet, abstraction wins out in these lonely paintings that Goldwater said "reject participation and draw into themselves."

The restrained palette in most of the last paintings—variations of gray deepened with brown, black, or ocher, and befogged whites— is related to Rothko's earlier technique of oppositions, but now the effect would be heavy, portentous, airless. The symbolic use of the mirrored shapes becomes demanding. A few years earlier Sollers could write on Rothko's more lyrical, chromatic paintings:

> It is not only the systole and diastole of the eye, contraction and dilation, but a symmetrical dialogue, rising-setting, East-West North-South, a disorientation, a re-polarization, a universal re-animation . . . The color is, so to speak, the veritable master-key of analogies, a sort of larger common denominator of a materialized communal passion: Unlike geometrical forms which push things into the back ground, it contains them. Rothko's

"living" rectangles, contradicted and juxtaposed with a dominant color create a veritable "realm."

This Heideggerean apprehension of Rothko's spaces, and his dialectical method, is basic to the whole oeuvre. No matter that in the last paintings a certain blunt opacity screens the experience. It is still an attempt to make a place, a realm, a country which, as Heidegger conceived it, is the function of the visual artist who must, from the beginning, face the eternal question: what is space? Profane spaces, he wrote, are always the privation of sacred spaces going far, far back. He asks:

> Is space one of the *Urphänomenen* [the primal phenomena] the contact with which, as Goethe thought, submerges a man—once he arrives at perceiving them—in a kind of apprehension that can even reach anguish? Because behind space, so it seems, there is nothing . . . And before it, there is no possible flight to anything else.[101]

This kind of spatial metaphysical anguish was already implicit in the large canvases that Rothko liked to call "tragic" and in which he denied the traditional functions of color. (What an irony that careless commentators still talk about his work as "color fields," a vulgar simplification that robs his achievement of its depth.) In the large works, as Andrew Forge has said, Rothko discovered that "a painting sufficiently large so that when you stand close, the edges are grayed off to one's peripheral vision, takes on a kind of presence in its surface that renders internal relationships irrelevant. The moment color and scale begin a dialogue, a close viewing range is like opening a door into an internal realm."[102] This, Forge thinks, is Rothko's grandeur, his limitation, his heaven and his hell.

The interior realm was where Rothko wished to or perhaps could only live, and what he hoped to express. The "theater of the mind," as Mallarmé called it, was immensely dramatic for Rothko. His darkness at the end did allude to the light of the theater in which, when the lights are gradually dimmed, expectation mounts urgently. Such darkness for Rothko was a crucible for imagination, even as he imagined terrible things. If his last two years were hellish, his paintings reflect them faithfully. It would be futile to see them as anything other than a mournful reckoning of his life's preoccupations, birth, dissolution, and death.

AFTERWORD

"It's a funny thing to say, but I mean for me they bring news. Which is not only in painting news. Every painting brings news—it's beyond the painting, right?"[103]

De Kooning's response to Rothko's later works was to the "news" that is beyond painting. For this Rothko would have been grateful. He was of the same generation and to some degree they had all worked with a sense of mission. If one accepts Kierkegaard's view of "the religious" aspect of a man's acts, then Rothko's enterprise was religious. He had begun life as a committed man. When he preached—for that is what he did in his public statements—he preached ethics. His Existentialist leanings eventually overcame his ambitions as a public missionary, but the *sense* of mission never left him. His view is apparent in his response to George Dennison's article "The Moral Effect of the Legend of Genet" published in 1967 in the first issue of *New American Review*. Dennison, who had frequently talked with Rothko during the late forties, had written about his work, and used to see him at long intervals in later years, writes:

> Mark said "I feel it has a bearing on our cause." I thought this
> was astute of him, since the aesthetics really were relevant but
> had been put entirely in literary and psychological terms. No one
> but he ever noticed their relevance to abstract art. But what was
> much more striking was his saying "our cause" since his col-
> leagues then were mostly rich, famous and dispersed.[104]

193

In Dennison's essay it is not difficult to discern the significance for Rothko. There are phrases scattered throughout that are typical of Rothko's way of thinking, such as a quote from *The Thief's Journal:*

> Was what I wrote true? False? Only this book of love will be real. What of the facts which served as its pretext? I must be their repository. It is not they which I am restoring.

"Such statements as these," Dennison wrote, "make clear to us at once that we cannot construe the 'I' of Genet as being, in the usual sense, the author himself. The books are presented overtly as a means of 'becoming'" (recalling Rothko's frequent statements that a painting lives by companionship, etc.). Dennison continues:

> This "I" then—the maker, the creator—is the common ground, or starting point, from which the voyage of dehumanization begins. To the extent that we accept or appropriate the "you" with which Genet addresses us, it is in response to this "I" alone, for all the others are transformations, chimeras of poetry and truth. Only the deeds of the maker are real, and they are not acts of crime, of loveless love and of betrayal, but acts of language, of shaping—and they are dazzling in their beauty.

It may well be that Rothko recognized himself in such lines.

A painter seeing Rothko's posthumous exhibition was reminded of something Malraux had said about paintings that are not religious, but are the opposite of profane. Was this Rothko's "cause"? And if it were, could it ever get past the modern barrier of irony? To paint the opposite of profane in an increasingly profane world was certainly a mission, and perhaps an impossible one. Yet, de Kooning perceived the message as beyond painting. Others, in experiencing awe or transport before his paintings, attributed them to a mystic. This was a repugnant idea to Rothko since it was *this* world he aspired to characterize. Yet it is obvious that he was ambivalent, and that there was another, more alluring world to which he was always drawn. He was like a mystic in that he had an overweaning private hunger for illumination, for personal enlightenment, for some direct experience—or at least the quality of that experience—with the transcendent. He was a mystic in the way Nietzsche described "a mystic soul . . . almost undecided whether it should communicate or conceal itself."

I believe it was this artful indecision, this purposeful equivocation that endowed Rothko's paintings with the power to draw us back. He heightened our attention by setting up an expectancy. When he hit his stride, as he did in the mid-fifties, he could surround us with large colored surfaces that both revealed and concealed. He knew how to stage a moment of stasis full of promise. I can remember entering the Janis Gallery and stopping in the center of the room. It was much as if I had entered a remote forest on a still day with nothing stirring, and heard, or imagined I heard, a single faint rustle somewhere. In the paintings there was always some all but invisible movement that I could never quite locate but that seemed to pervade the whole. And, just as in the forest I would stand attentively, every nerve mobilized, waiting for the next sound, seeking its source, so before Rothko's paintings I would await, or summon, an indication of source. The movement Rothko created was always hovering, respiring, pulsing, but never wholly described. He teased his viewer into a state of receptivity and inquiry. Unaccustomed juxtapositions of huge areas of color (or sometimes merely tone) challenged not only the eyes of the beholder but his entire psychological and motor being. Rothko's uncanny command of these often baffling juxtapositions and subtle movements transformed his viewer into more than a collaborator. If his soul was almost undecided whether to communicate or reveal itself, its movements were nonetheless suggestive. It was this very equivocation that gave back so much that had been banished from painting—a chance for metaphor, a chance for indeterminate feeling, a chance for mystery.

There was certainly a pronounced hermetic element in Rothko's oeuvre that excited some and irritated others. All kinds of explanations were summoned. Butor even goes so far as to suggest that Rothko's development occurred during the height of the McCarthy era, and that this played a role since Rothko "produces an oasis of light that protects him and judges everything else, a light intended to benefit only individuals, in secret." This Butor regards as an escape. But he forgets that many painters have responded to their time with immense indignation which is not at all endemic to their art. Pissarro, for instance, seethed with anger about unjust social conditions, yet construed a calm, evenly lighted world of delectation. It was in his temperament, just as the longing for a universal experience of unity was in Rothko's. When Rothko insisted on the materialistic base of his art, refusing mysticism, he defended himself against the abyss, declaring again and again that these are the visible facts of his existence that includes all adjectives—from joyful to sorrowful, from earthly to transcendent. Yet the desire to be ravished, quite as the mystics desired to be ravished, was always there.

The frequent allusion to Rothko's silences in critical response bear out the approach to his work that sees it as the opposite of profane. Religiousness and reverent silence are traditionally associated. Yet, which culture can prepare the viewer for such silence? It is certainly an anomaly in our own. Rothko rightly sensed that such work would find only very sensitive viewers and limited understanding. To understand his impulse would perhaps require some other context, far removed from the modern; a leap back into a state of mind utterly diverse from the modern. If his was a hidden dream of some sacred enclosure, it is better considered in the context of some very distant dream, such as that of the 12th-century monk Theophilus who wrote to an imaginary apprentice of the spirit of wisdom, understanding, counsel, fortitude, knowledge, and godliness:

> Animated, dearest son, by these supporting virtues, you have approached the House of God with confidence, and have adorned it with so much beauty; you have embellished the ceilings or walls with varied work in different colours and have, in some measure, shown to beholders the paradise of God, glowing with various flowers, verdant with herbs and foliage, and cherishing with crowns of varying merit the souls of the saints. You have given them cause to praise the Creator in the creature and proclaim Him wonderful in His works. For the human eye is not able to consider on what work first to fix its gaze; if it beholds the ceilings they glow like brocades; if it considers the walls they are a kind of paradise; if it regards the profusion of light from the windows, it marvels at the inestimable beauty of the glass and the infinitely rich and various workmanship . . .[105]

The problem of light obsessing Rothko can be seen better in other contexts. The light he craved was a light of revelation, quite literally, and it had to be concealed. Emanation was essential. Beneath his preoccupation were endless speculations of the kind Maurice Blanchot, à propos of Nietzsche, posed when he asks: why this imperialism of light? "Light illuminates, that is to say that light hides itself, that is its sly characteristic. Light illuminates: that which is illuminated presents itself in an immediate presence which reveals itself without revealing that which manifests it. Light effaces its traces; invisible, it renders visible."[106] The paradox implicit in Rothko's best work is that he wished also to name the light itself and not only the things it illuminated. How often in his later works there are flares of burning light, sparks that glow uncannily, sparks that seem fraught with very old associations dredged up from the mythic world in which Rothko was once immersed. These are more like the sparks in the original Book of the Zohar. Matti Megged has written that the main concerns of the Zohar, or the Book of Splendour, are the mysteries of the emanation of the divine powers of the hidden God. "On the one hand, the God himself, the Ein-Sof, is so remote from human understanding that nothing can be said about him. On the other, the whole *raison d'être* of the Kabbalah, and probably of any mysticism, is the need to grasp, by thought and imagination, the living, dynamic presence of God in the world."[107] Out of this contradiction, he writes, the author of the Zohar strived to find the language appropriate to the expression of things he knew and admitted could not be talked about:

> Here lies the tremendously powerful poetic imagination of the author. He finds words, terms, metaphors whose purpose is to express the inexpressible such as: "A spark of darkness emerged-but-not-emerged from the obscurest of obscure, from the secret of Ein-Sof, not white and not dark, not red and not green, without any color at all . . ." And from this spark, within-in-within, emerged one fountain from which all nether entities got their colors.

The Book of Zohar, then, is best received as a high order of poetry, and perhaps the same must be felt about Rothko's late works. "They are not paintings," he said.

Rothko was a man of culture, in the precise sense of culture designed by the 20th century as the opposite of, or at least different from, nature. "Culture," wrote Leopold von Wiese in 1939, "is above all not 'an order of phenomena' and is not to be found in the worlds of perceptible or conceived things. It does not belong to the world of substance; it is part of the world of values, of which it is a formal category . . . Culture is no more a thing-concept than 'plus,' 'higher,' or 'better.'" Sartre, in his summing up in "The Words," thought that "Culture doesn't save anything or anyone; it doesn't justify. But it is a product of man: he projects himself into it, he recognizes himself in it; that critical mirror alone offers him his image." In the light of both these definitions of culture Rothko was a man of culture. His mission was to go beyond the world of substances to a world, literally, of values. His experience, or the experience he deemed worthy of expression, was of things and thoughts man has made. He was making a language to cover certain kinds of experiences called passions or emotions that rise up in self-reflecting modern psyches, but that have an immemorial history in art. Rothko's painting culture embraced a wide spectrum of experiences, but all reflected his respect for the expression of the longing for transcendence: from the artists of Torcello and Ravenna to Fra Angelico, to Rembrandt, to Turner—all. Knowledge was the goal, even knowledge of the seemingly unknowable. Rembrandt remained one of Rothko's beacons—Rembrandt who knew the importance of feeling rooted in the everyday world of human emotion, and yet wished to transcend it; Rembrandt who his contemporary Joachim van Sandrart said did not hesitate to oppose or contradict the rules of art, and demanded "universal harmony." There is a late portrait in the Kimbell Art Museum in Fort Worth, of a young Jewish scholar in which Rembrandt unmistakably speaks of this tension. The young man gazes from his dark atmosphere, one eye engaged with the vision of this world, the other, shadowed, rapt in another.[108]

Rothko said he looked forward to a time when an artist would be rewarded for the meaning of his life's work. The meaning of his own life's work may emerge more clearly, or at least, differently, in the future. What it meant to many of his contemporaries is expressed in a memorial statement by Andrew Carnduff Ritchie:

> One cannot escape the feeling, avoiding all the current psycho-analytic jargon in art criticism, that there was in Rothko, raised to a pitch of poetic intensity, a Zoroastrian sense of light and darkness as symbols of goodness and evil, growing out of an inheritance from a youth spent in virgin Oregon, merging with memories of his Old Testament ancestors and a deep recall of his origins in that great land of opposites, Russia.[109]

NOTES

1. "The Romantics Were Prompted," *Possibilities,* Vol. I, Winter 1947/48.
2. Conversation with the author, January 1957.
3. Author's conversation with Moise, Rothko's older brother, 1971.
4. *Contemporary Painters* (New York: Museum of Modern Art, 1948).
5. *Essays on Art,* New York: Rudge, 1916.
6. I am indebted to Professor Rudolf Arnheim for information on Cizek.
7. "Commemorative Essay," Jan. 7, 1965, in *Milton Avery* (Greenwich, Conn.: New York Graphic Society, 1969).
8. Conversation with author, Feb. 4, 1972.
9. Interview on file at Archives of American Art.
10. "On Regionalism," *American Art, 1700-1960, Sources and Documents* (Englewood Cliffs: Prentice-Hall, 1965), p. 202.
11. Interview, 1972.
12. Gerald M. Monroe, "Art Front," *Archives of American Art Journal,* Vol. 13, No. 3, 1973.
13. Statement, catalogue for group exhibition at the David Porter Gallery, Washington, D.C., 1945.
14. Conversation with the author, 1969.
15. "Ulysses, Order and Myth," *The Dial,* November 1923.
16. *An Essay on Man* (New Haven: Yale University Press, 1944).
17. Sidney Janis, *Abstract and Surrealist Art in America* (New York: Reynal and Hitchcock, 1944).
18. *The Birth of Tragedy,* translated by Walter Kaufmann (New York: Vintage, 1967).
19. *The Portable Nietzsche* (New York: Viking, 1954).
20. *The Tiger's Eye,* October 1949.
21. First Annual Membership Exhibition Catalogue, 16-29, Rockefeller Center, New York, 1937.
22. "Nature of Abstract Art," *Marxist Quarterly,* Jan.-March 1937.

23. Thomas B. Hess, *Barnett Newman* (New York, The Museum of Modern Art, 1971).
24. Holograph ms. in Keats-Shelley House, Piazza di Spagna, Rome.
25. "Pollock Symposium," *Art News*, April 1967.
26. Catalogue for group exhibition at the David Porter Gallery, Washington, D.C., 1945.
27. John Hultberg in *A Period of Exploration, San Francisco, 1945-50* by Mary Fuller McChesney (Oakland Museum, 1973).
28. Conversation with author, 1958.
29. *New Republic*, April 24, 1944.
30. Hess, *Barnett Newman.*
31. "Jan. 17, 1947," *Ararat*, 12, Fall, 1971.
32. *The Tiger's Eye*, Dec. 15, 1948.
33. *Barnett Newman* (New York: Abrams 1978).
34. *The Truants* (New York, Anchor/Doubleday, 1982).
35. Rilke, "First Duino Elegy."
36. "The Romantics Were Prompted," *Possibilities.*
37. *Notes of a Painter*, 1908.
38. "Looking at Life with the Eyes of a Child, 1955," in Jack D. Flam, *Matisse on Art* (New York: Dutton, 1978).
39. "Interview with Eugène Tardieu," *Echo de Paris*, May 13, 1895.
40. "The Romantics Were Prompted," *Possibilities*, I.
41. Translated by B. Frechtman (New York: Philosophical Library, 1947).
42. "Indirect Language and the Voices of Silence" in *Signs* (Chicago: Northwestern University Press, 1964), p. 44.
43. Bradford Cook, *Selected Prose Poems, Essays and Letters* (Baltimore: Johns Hopkins University Press, 1956).
44. "Eye and Mind," *The Primary of Perception* (Chicago: Northwestern University Press, 1964), p. 178.
45. *Interiors*, Vol. 110, May 1951, p. 104.
46. "Eye and Mind."
47. "Indirect Language and the Voices of Silence," p. 52.
48. Conversation with the author, January 1957.
49. Jean-Paul Sartre, *Situations II* (Paris: Gallimard, 1948).
50. "Indirect Language and the Voices of Silence."
51. Unpublished doctoral dissertation, Princeton University, 1951.
52. Lippold papers, Archives of American Art.
53. Susanne K. Langer, *Feeling and Form* (New York: Scribner, 1953).
54. Interview with Betty Parsons, Archives of American Art.
55. Lee Seldes, *The Legacy of Mark Rothko* (New York: Holt, Rinehart and Winston, 1978).
56. Conversation with the author.
57. Quoted in press release of Art Institute of Chicago.
58. DeKooning, "Two Americans in Action."
59. *Time*, March 3, 1961.
60. Homage prepared to be read to members of the National Institute of Arts and Letters, January 1971.

61. "A Lecture on Something," *It Is,* no. 4, Autumn, 1959.
62. Author's transcription, partially published in *The New York Times,* Oct. 31, 1958.
63. "Mark Rothko: Portrait of the Artist as an Angry Man," *Harper's,* Vol. 24, #1422, July 1970.
64. Giulio Carlo Argan, "Fra Angelico" (Skira, 1955; Cleveland: World Publishing Co.).
65. Ibid.
66. Conversation with the author, Winter 1959.
67. D. Ashton on "Philosophy of Stanley Kunitz," *The New York Times,* Dec. 10, 1959.
68. Letter to the author, March 9, 1959.
69. "A Symposium on How To Combine Architecture, Painting and Sculpture," *Interiors,* Vol. 10, May 1951.
70. "Mark Rothko," broadcast created by Dore Ashton for Canadian Broadcasting Co.
71. Tate Report, 1968-1970.
72. *Art Digest,* November 1954.
73. Catalogue foreword, Contemporary Arts Museum, Houston, Sept. 5, 1957.
74. *Chicago Art Institute Quarterly,* Nov. 15, 1954.
75. *Quadrum,* no. 10, 1961.
76. "Reflections on the Rothko Exhibition," *Arts,* no. 35; March 1961.
77. Conversation with the author.
78. Conversation with the author.
79. "The Rothko Chapel," *Art Journal,* Vol. XXX, no. 3, Spring, 1971.
80. Werner Jaeger, *Early Christianity and Greek Paideia* (Cambridge: Harvard University Press, 1965).
81. David Sutherland Wallace-Hadrill, *The Greek Patristic View of Nature* (Manchester University Press, 1968).
82. Kurt Weitzmann, *The Age of Spirituality* (The Metropolitan Museum of Art in association with Princeton University Press, 1980).
83. "Working with Rothko," *New American Review,* No. 12, 1971.
84. "Crippled Symmetry," RES 2, Harvard College, Autumn 1981.
85. Conversation with Motherwell, March 28, 1967.
86. Flam, *Matisse on Art.*
87. Catalogue for Rothko exhibition, Kunsthaus, Zürich, March 21-May 9, 1971.
88. All quotes from conversations with the author.
89. *Spectator,* March 7, 1970.
90. "The Rothko Chapel," *Art Journal,* Vol. XXX, No. 3, Spring 1971.
91. Canadian Broadcasting Company broadcast prepared by author.
92. *Modern Painting and the Northern Romantic Tradition* (New York: Harper and Row, 1975).
93. "The Rothko Chapel," *Art in America,* Vol. 61, no. 1, Jan.-Feb. 1973.
94. Press release from *Rothko Chapel* for Concert, April 9, 1972.
95. Letter to the author, April 29, 1982.

96. Conversation with the author.
97. Motherwell notes, April 21, 1969.
98. "The Mosques of New York, or The Art of Mark Rothko," *New World Writing*, no. 21, 1962.
99. *Art de France*, no. 4, 1964.
100. "Rothko's Black Paintings," *Art in America*, Vol. 59, no. 2, March-April 1971.
101. *L'Art et l'espace* (St. Gallen: Erker-Verlag, 1969).
102. Conversation with the author, August, 1982.
103. "Interview with Joseph Liss," *Art News*, January 1979.
104. Letter to the author, Sept. 27, 1978.
105. Translated by C. R. Dodwell, Theophilus, *The Various Arts* (London: Thomas Nelson and Sons Ltd., 1961).
106. L'Entretien infini (Paris: Gallimard, 1969).
107. Matti Megged, *The Darkened Light* (Tel Aviv: Sifryat Poalim, 1981).
108. This painting is surpassingly paradoxical. The worldly eye is becalmed, somewhat cool, while the visionary eye springs from its shadowy depths with intense, very palpable light. The two suspended realms—inner and outer, or spiritual and mundane—are pronouncedly different. Yet the picture as a whole can be perceived as harmonious.
109. *Salute to Mark Rothko*, Yale University Gallery, May 66-June 20, 1971.

SELECTED BIBLIOGRAPHY

I   GENERAL AND BACKGROUND MATERIAL

Argan, Giulio Carlo. *Fra Angelico*. Geneva: Skira, 1955.

Ashton, Dore. *The New York School: A Cultural Reckoning*. New York: Viking, 1972.

————. *A Reading of Modern Art*. Cleveland: Press of Case Western Reserve Univ., 1969.

————. *The Unknown Shore: A View of Contemporary Art*. Boston: Little, Brown, 1962.

————. *Yes, but . . . : A Critical Study of Philip Guston*. New York: Viking, 1976.

Blanchot, Maurice. *L'Entretien infini*. Paris: Gallimard, 1969.

Breeskin, Adelyn D. *Milton Avery*. Washington, D.C.: National Collection of Fine Arts, 1969.

Cage, John "A Lecture on Something." *It Is*, no. 4 (Autumn 1959): 73-78. (On Morton Feldman.)

Feldman, Morton. "After Modernism." *Art in America* 59 (November-December 1971): 68-77.

————. "Crippled Symmetry." *RES* 2 (Autumn 1981): 91-103.

Flam, Jack D. *Matisse on Art*. New York: Dutton, 1978.

Geldzahler, Henry. *American Painting in the Twentieth Century*. New York: Metropolitan Museum of Art, 1965.

Haskell, Barbara. *Milton Avery*. New York: Whitney Museum, 1982.

Heidegger, Martin. *Die Kunst und der Raum; L'Art et l'espace*. St. Gallen: Erker-Verlag, 1969.

Hess, Thomas B. *Abstract Painting: Background and American Phase*. New York: Viking, 1951.

————. *Barnett Newman*. New York: Museum of Modern Art, 1971.

Jaeger, Werner. *Early Christianity and Greek Paideia*. Cambridge, Mass.: Harvard Univ. Press, 1965.

Janis, Sidney. *Abstract and Surrealist Art in America*. New York: Reynal and Hitchcock, 1944.

MacNaughton, Mary Davis, and Lawrence Alloway. *Adolph Gottlieb: A Retrospective*. New York: Arts Publishers, 1981.

Megged, Matti. *The Darkened Light*. Tel Aviv: Sifryat Poalim, 1981.

Merleau-Ponty, Maurice. *The Primacy of Perception*. Evanston, Ill.: Northwestern Univ. Press, 1964.

————. *Signs*. Evanston, Ill.: Northwestern Univ. Press, 1964.

O'Doherty, Brian. *American Masters: The Voice and the Myth*. New York: Random House, 1973.

O'Neill, John, ed. *Clyfford Still*. New York: Metropolitan Museum of Art, 1979.

Rilke, Rainer Maria. *Duino Elegies*. Translated by J. B. Leishman and Stephen Spender. New York: Norton, 1939.

Rosenberg, Harold. *Artworks and Packages*. New York: Horizon Press, 1969.

————. *The De-Definition of Art*. New York: Horizon Press, 1972.

Rosenblum, Robert. *Modern Painting and the Northern Romantic Tradition: Friedrich to Rothko*. New York: Harper and Row, 1975.

Sandler, Irving. *The Triumph of American Painting: A History of Abstract Expressionism*. New York: Praeger, 1970.

Sartre, Jean-Paul. *Situations II*. Paris: Gallimard, 1948.

Seitz, William C. "Abstract Expressionist Painting in America: An Interpretation Based on the Work and Thought of Six Key Figures." Ph.D. dissertation, Princeton University, 1955.

Solman, Joseph. "The Easel Division of the WPA Federal Art Project." In *New Deal Art Projects: An Anthology of Memoirs*. Edited by Francis V. O'Connor. Washington, D.C.: Smithsonian Inst. Press, 1972.

Sylvester, David, ed. *Modern Art: From Fauvism to Abstract Expressionism*. New York: Franklin Watts, 1966.

Theophilus. *The Various Arts*. Translated and edited by C. R. Dodwell. London: Thomas Nelson, 1961.

Wallace-Hadrill, David Sutherland. *The Greek Patristic View of Nature*. Manchester: Manchester Univ. Press, 1968.

Weitzmann, Kurt. *The Age of Spirituality*. New York: Metropolitan Museum of Art, 1980.

II   SELECTED EXHIBITION CATALOGS AND REVIEWS

Ashton, Dore. "Art." *Arts and Architecture* 75 (April 1958): 8, 29, 32.

————. "Lettre de New York." *Cimaise*, ser. 5, no. 4 (March-April 1958): 30-31.

Bowness, Alan. "Absolutely Abstract." *Observer* (London), 15 October 1961, p. 27.

Bulletin of the Museum of Art, Portland [Oregon] 3 (November-December 1933): n. pag.

Crehan, Hubert. "Rothko's Wall of Light: A Show of His New Work at Chicago." *Arts Digest* 29 (November 1, 1954): 5, 19.

Fifteen Americans. New York: Museum of Modern Art, 1952.

Goldwater, Robert. "Reflections on the Rothko Exhibition." *Arts* 35 (March 1961): 42-45.
Hess, Thomas B. "Rothko: A Venetian Souvenir." *Art News* 69 (November 1970): 40-41, 72-74.
Hunter, Sam. "Diverse Modernism." *New York Times,* 14 March 1948, sec. 2, p. x8.
————. Text on Rothko for *Lipton, Rothko, Smith, and Tobey.* Venice: *XXIX Exposizione Biennale Internazionale d'Arte,* 1958.
J. L. "Three Moderns: Rothko, Gromaire and Solman." *Art News* 38 (January 20, 1940): 12.
Kainen, Jacob. "Our Expressionists." *Art Front* 3 (February 1937): 14-15.
Kuh, Katharine. "Mark Rothko." *Art Institute of Chicago Quarterly* 48 (November 15, 1954): 68.
McKinney, Donald. *Mark Rothko.* Zürich: Kunsthaus Zürich, 1971.
Mark Rothko Paintings. New York: Art of This Century, 1945.
The New American Painting. New York: Museum of Modern Art, 1959.
The New York School: The First Generation, Paintings of the 1940's and 1950's. Los Angeles: Los Angeles County Museum of Art, 1965.
O'Doherty, Brian. "Art: Rothko Panels Seen." *New York Times,* April 10, 1963, p. 36.
Perocco, Guido. *Mark Rothko.* Venice: Museo d'Arte Moderno Ca'Pesaro, 1970.
Pleynet, Marcelin. "Exposition Mark Rothko." *Tel Quel,* no. 12 (Winter 1963): 39-41.
Riley, Maude. "The Mythical Rothko and His Myths." *Arts Digest* 19 (January 15, 1945): 15.
Ritchie, Andrew Carnduff. *Salute to Mark Rothko.* New Haven: Yale University Art Gallery, 1971.
Rosenblum, Robert. *Mark Rothko: The Surrealist Years.* New York: Pace Gallery, 1981.
Russell, John. "A Grand Achievement of the Fifties." *Sunday Times* (London), October 15, 1961, p. 39.
Selz, Peter. *Mark Rothko.* New York: Museum of Modern Art, 1961.
Waldemar-Geroge. *The Ten.* Paris: Galerie Bonaparte, 1936.
Waldman, Diane. *Mark Rothko: A Retrospective.* New York: Guggenheim Museum/Abrams, 1978.

III   ARTICLES ON ROTHKO

Alloway, Lawrence. "Notes on Rothko." *Art International* 6 (1962): 90-94.
Ashton, Dore. "Art: Lecture by Rothko." *New York Times,* October 31, 1958, p. 26.
————. "L'Automne à New York: Letter from New York." *Cimaise,* ser. 6, no. 2 (December 1958): 37-40.
————. "Mark Rothko." *Arts and Architecture* 74 (August 1957): 8, 31.
————. "Oranges and Lemons, An Adjustment." *Arts Magazine* 51 (February 1977): 142.
————. "The Rothko Chapel in Houston." *Studio* 181 (June 1971): 272-75.

Butor, Michel. "The Mosques of New York, or The Art of Mark Rothko." In *New World Writing*, no. 21. Philadelphia: Lippincott, 1962.

De Kooning, Elaine. "Two Americans in Action: Franz Kline and Mark Rothko." *Art News Annual* 27 (1958): 86-97, 174-179.

De Menil, Dominique (Mrs. John de Menil). "Address given in the Rothko Chapel, 26 February 1971." Transcript on deposit in Rothko file, Whitney Museum, New York.

Dennison, George. "The Painting of Mark Rothko." Unpublished, n.d. On deposit in Rothko file, Museum of Modern Art, New York.

Drudi, Gabriella. "Mark Rothko." *Appia* 2 (January 1960): n. pag.

Edwards, Roy, and Ralph Pomeroy. "Working with Rothko." In *New American Review*, no. 12. New York: Simon and Schuster, 1971.

Fischer, John. "Mark Rothko: Portrait of the Artist as an Angry Man." *Harper's*, July 1970, pp. 16-23.

Goldwater, Robert. "Rothko's Black Paintings." *Art in America* 59 (March-April 1971): 58-63.

Liss, Joseph. "Portrait by Rothko." Unpublished, n.d. On deposit in Rothko file, Whitney Museum, New York.

MacAgy, Douglas. "Mark Rothko." *Magazine of Art* 42 (January 1949): 20-21.

O'Doherty, Brian. "Rothko." *Art International* 14 (October 20, 1970): 30-44.

————. "The Rothko Chapel." *Art in America* 61 (January-February 1973): 14-18, 20.

Oeri, Georgine. "Mark Rothko." *Quadrum*, no. 10 (1961): 65-74.

————. "Tobey and Rothko." *Baltimore Museum of Art News Quarterly* 23 (Winter 1960): 2-8.

Putnam, Wallace. "Mark Rothko Told Me." *Arts Magazine* 48 (April 1974): 44-45.

Sollers, Philippe. "Le mur du sens." *Art de France* 4 (1964): 239-251.

IV   ARTICLES AND STATEMENTS BY ROTHKO
      (ARRANGED CHRONOLOGICALLY)

[Statement.] In *The Ten: Whitney Dissenters*. New York: Mercury Galleries, 1938. (With Bernard Bradden.)

[Letter.] In Edward Alden Jewell, "The Realm of Art: A New Platform and Other Matters: 'Globalism' Pops into View." *New York Times*, June 13, 1943, p. x9. (With Adolph Gottlieb and probable collaboration of Barnett Newman.)

"The Portrait and the Modern Artist." WNYC radio broadcast "Art in New York," October 13, 1943. (With Adolph Gottlieb; excerpts from transcript in *The New York School*, Los Angeles County Museum of Art, 1965.)

"Personal Statement." In *A Painting Prophecy—1950*. Washington, D.C.: David Porter Gallery, 1945.

"Clyfford Still." In *Clyfford Still*. New York: Art of This Century, 1946.

"The Ides of Art: 'The Attitudes of 10 Artists on Their Art and Contemporaneousness." *The Tiger's Eye* (December 1947): 44.

"The Romantics Were Prompted." *Possibilities* 1 (Winter 1947-48): 84.

"Statement on His Attitude in Painting." *The Tiger's Eye* (October 1949): 114.

"A Symposium on How To Combine Architecture, Painting and Sculpture." *Interiors* 110 (May 1951): 104.

Unpublished letter to Lloyd Goodrich, Director, Whitney Museum of American Art, New York. December 20, 1952. On deposit in Rothko file, Whitney Museum.

Unpublished letter to Rosalind Irvine, Whitney Museum of American Art, New York, April 9, 1957. On deposit in Rothko file, Whitney Museum.

"Editor's Letters." *Art News* 56 (December 1957): 6.

[Interview with Rothko.] In Selden Rodman, *Conversations with Artists*. New York: Devin-Adair, 1957.

[Lecture.] Delivered Fall 1958, Pratt Institute, Brooklyn. Excerpts from transcript in *The New York School*, Los Angeles County Museum of Art.

Eulogy for Milton Avery. Delivered January 7, 1965, New York Society for Ethical Culture, New York. Transcript published in Breeskin, *Milton Avery*.

ILLUSTRATIONS

8. *The Omen of the Eagle*   1942
   oil on canvas 25¾ x 17¾ in.
   Photo Quesada/Burke, courtesy The Mark Rothko Foundation, New York

9. *Subway (Subterranean Fantasy)*   c.1938
   oil on canvas 34⁵⁄₁₆ x 46½ in.
   Photo Quesada/Burke, courtesy The Mark Rothko Foundation, New York

10. Untitled   c.1936
    oil on canvas 32 x 42 in.
    © Estate of Mark Rothko
    Photo courtesy The Solomon R. Guggenheim Museum, New York

11. *Subway Scene*   1938
    oil on canvas 35 x 47¼ in.
    © Estate of Mark Rothko
    Photo courtesy Dr. Kate Rothko Prizel

12. Untitled   c.1936
    oil on canvas 16¹⁄₁₆ x 20¹⁄₁₆ in.
    Courtesy The Mark Rothko Foundation, New York

13. *Antigone*   1938-41
    oil on canvas 34⁵⁄₁₆ x 46¼ in.
    Courtesy The Mark Rothko Foundation, New York

14. JOAN MIRO
    The Hunter (Catalan Landscape)   1923-24
    oil on canvas 25½ x 39½ in.
    Courtesy Collection, The Museum of Modern Art, New York. Purchase

15. *Horizontal Phantom*   1943
    oil on canvas 35¾ x 47¾ in.
    © Estate of Mark Rothko
    Photo courtesy The Pace Gallery, New York

16. *The Syrian Bull*   1943
    oil on canvas 39½ x 27½ in.
    Photo David Preston, courtesy Collection Annalee Newman

17. *Hierarchical Birds*   c.1944
    oil on canvas 39⅝ x 31⅝ in.
    Photo Quesada/Burke, courtesy The Mark Rothko Foundation, New York

18 *Poised Elements*   1944
    oil on canvas 36 x 48 in.
    © Estate of Mark Rothko
    Photo courtesy The Pace Gallery, New York

19. *Olympian Play*   c.1944
    oil on canvas 19⅝ x 27⁹⁄₁₆ in.
    Courtesy The Mark Rothko Foundation, New York

20. Untitled 1945
    oil on canvas 39¼ x 27¼ in.
    © Estate of Mark Rothko
    Photo courtesy The Pace Gallery, New York

21. Untitled 1949
    watercolor, tempera on paper 39⅞ x 25⅞ in., image; 40⅟₁₆ x 26⅝ in., sheet
    Photo Quesada/Burke, courtesy The Mark Rothko Foundation, New York

22. Untitled c. 1946
    oil on canvas 39⅜ x 27⁹⁄₁₆ in.
    Courtesy The Mark Rothko Foundation, New York

23. Mark Rothko at Betty Parsons Gallery, New York, 1949
    Photo courtesy Aaron Siskind

24. *Number 22* 1949
    oil on canvas 117 x 107⅛ in.
    Photo Geoffrey Clements, courtesy Collection, The Museum of Modern
    Art, New York. Gift of the artist

25. *Number 27* 1954
    oil on canvas 81 x 86⅝ in.
    Courtesy Collection Anne W. Sowell, Fort Worth

26. *Number 9* 1958
    oil on canvas 99 x 82 in.
    Courtesy Collection Mr. and Mrs. Donald Blinken

27. Untitled c.1944-46
    watercolor, ink on paper 22⅛ x 30¹³⁄₁₆ in. image; 22¾ x 31⁵⁄₁₆ in., sheet
    Photo Quesada/Burke, courtesy The Mark Rothko Foundation, New York

28. *Triptych* from the Harvard Murals 1962
    oil on canvas left panel 104⅞ x 117 in.; central panel 104⅞ x 180½ in.;
    right panel 104⅞ x 96 in.
    Courtesy the President and Fellows of Harvard College

29. Mark Rothko on his birthday in 1960
    © Estate of Mark Rothko
    Photo Regina Bogat, courtesy The Pace Gallery, New York

30. Rothko, Carlo Battaglia, Christopher, and Mell in Rome, 1966
    Photo courtesy Carla Panicali

Interior 1932/1935
oil on masonite $23^{15}/_{16} \times 18^5/_{16}$ in.
Gift of The Mark Rothko Foundation, © 1995 Board of Trustees, National
Gallery of Art, Washington

Slow Swirl by the Edge of the Sea 1944
oil on canvas $75^3/_8 \times 84^3/_4$ in.
The Museum of Modern Art, New York. Bequest of Mrs. Mark Rothko
through The Mark Rothko Foundation, Inc. Photograph © 1996 The Museum
of Modern Art, New York

Number 18 1948–49
oil on canvas $67^1/_4 \times 55^7/_8$ in.
Frances Lehman Loeb Art Center, Vassar College, Poughkeepsie, New York.
Gift of Mrs. John D. Rockefeller 3rd (Blanchette Hooker, class of 1931)

Number 18 1951
oil on canvas $81^3/_4 \times 67$ in.
Munson-Williams-Proctor Institute, Museum of Art, Utica, New York, Museum
Purchase (Copyright, Rothko Estate)

Blue over Orange 1956
oil on canvas 86×79 in.
Collection Mr. and Mrs. Donald Blinken

The Rothko Room
The Tate Gallery, London

Number 117 1961
oil on canvas 93×81 in.
Collection Mr. and Mrs. Donald Blinken

Number 17 1947
oil on canvas $48 \times 35^7/_8$ in.
The Solomon R. Guggenheim Museum, New York, Gift of The Mark Rothko
Foundation, 1986, Photograph by David Heald © The Solomon R. Guggenheim
Foundation, New York

BRIEF CHRONOLOGY

1903   Born Marcus Rothkowitz, September 25, in Dvinsk, Russia.

1913   Settles in the United States with mother and sister in Portland, Oregon, August 17.

1921   Graduates from high school and wins scholarship to Yale University, where he remains until 1923. Moves to New York.

1924   Enrolls at the Art Students' League, January 1924. Returns to Portland where he joins a theater company.

1925   Returns to New York and enrolls in Max Weber's classes at the League; remains a member until 1929.

1928   First exhibition in a group show at the Opportunity Galleries, New York, November 15–December 12. Becomes friendly with Milton Avery.

1929   Takes part-time job teaching children at the Center Academy, Brooklyn Jewish Center; remains on faculty until 1952. Meets Adolph Gottlieb.

1932   Marries Edith Sachar.

1933   First one-man exhibition at the Museum of Art, Portland, Oregon, of his own drawings and watercolors and those of his pupils, summer. First one-man show in New York at the Contemporary Arts Gallery, November 21.

1934   Among 200 members at inauguration of Artists' Union

1935   Helps form the group "The Ten." Group's first exhibition at the Montross Gallery, New York, December 16–January 4.

1936   A founding member of American Artists' Congress. Meets Barnett Newman. Shows with "The Ten" at Galerie Bonaparte, Paris, November 10–24. Joins easel division of WPA, until 1939.

1938   Becomes United States citizen. Shows in "The Ten: Whitney Dissenters" at the Mercury Galleries, New York, November 5–26.

1940   Shows together with Marcel Gromaire and Joseph Solman at the Neumann-Willard Gallery, New York, January 8–27, and begins to sign his works Mark Rothko. Founding member of the Federation of Modern Painters and Sculptors.

1943   Third Annual Federation of Modern Painters and Sculptors Exhibition at Wildenstein Galleries, New York, June 3–26. In response to negative criticism in the *New York Times*, writes letter with Adolph Gottlieb, June 7, published June 13.

1944   Meets Mary Alice Beistle, called Mell.

1945   First one-man show at Peggy Guggenheim's Art of This Century Gallery, New York, January 9–February 4. Divorces Edith Sachar and marries Mell. Included in "A Painting Prophecy, 1950" at the David Porter Gallery, Washington, D.C., in February.

1946   Writes catalogue foreword for Clyfford Still's first one-man exhibition at the Art of This Century Gallery, New York, February 12–March 7. Exhibits watercolors at the Mortimer Brandt Gallery, New York, April 22–May 4. Spends summer in East Hampton. Shows oils and watercolors in one-man exhibition at the San Francisco Museum, August 16–September 8. Part of show travels to Santa Barbara Museum. Becomes friendly with Robert Motherwell.

1947   One-man show at the Betty Parsons Gallery, New York. Shows annually there until 1952. Visiting instructor at the California School of Fine Arts, June 23–August 1.

1948   With Clyfford Still, Robert Motherwell, William Baziotes, and David Hare, founds the school called "Subjects of the Artist."

1949   Returns to the California School of Fine Arts as guest instructor, July 5–August 12. Included in "The Intrasubjectives" at the Samuel M. Kootz Gallery, September 15–October 3.

1950   Spring trip to England, France, and Italy. Joins seventeen other painters and ten sculptors in protest letter to the Metropolitan Museum of Art (dated May 20). A photograph published in *Life* magazine the following January earns the group the title "The Irascibles." Daughter Kathy Lynn (Kate) born December 30.

1951   Appointed Assistant Professor, Department of Design, Brooklyn College. Remains until June 1954.

1952   Included in "Fifteen Americans" exhibition at the Museum of Modern Art, New York, March 25–June 11, organized by Dorothy C. Miller.

1954   One-man exhibition at the Art Institute of Chicago, October 18–December 31, later shown in part at the Rhode Island School of Design.

1955   First of two one-man shows at the Sidney Janis Gallery, New York, April 11–May 14.

216

1957   Visiting artist, Tulane University, New Orleans, February–March.

1958   One of four Americans represented with one-man shows at the XXIX Biennale in Venice, June 14–October 19. Commissioned by architect Philip Johnson to paint murals for Seagram Building. Travels to Italy, France, Belgium, the Netherlands, and England. Lecture at Pratt Institute, Brooklyn in October, reported by Dore Ashton in the *New York Times* and in French magazine *Cimaise*. Refuses Guggenheim award for American section in Guggenheim International Award exhibition, New York, October 22–February 23.

1960   One-man exhibition at the Phillips Collection, Washington, D.C., May 4–31.

1961   One-man exhibition at the Museum of Modern Art, New York, January 12–March 12. Exhibition travels until 1963 to London, Amsterdam, Basel, Rome, and Paris. Receives commission from the Society of Fellows, Harvard University, for murals for the Holyoke Center.

1963   Exhibition of "Five Mural Panels Executed for Harvard University by Mark Rothko" at the Solomon R. Guggenheim Museum, New York, April 9–June 2. Son Christopher Hall born August 31.

1964   Receives commission from Dominique and John de Menil for murals for Catholic Chapel in Houston, later changed to an ecumenical chapel. Spends summer in Amagansett, Long Island.

1965   Awarded the Brandeis University Creative Arts Medal, March 28.

1966   Travels with wife and two children to Italy, France, the Netherlands, Belgium, and England, spring.

1967   Teaches summer session at the University of California in Berkeley.

1968   Stricken with a serious aneurysm of the aorta. Becomes member of the National Institute of Arts and Letters, May 28. Spends summer in Provincetown, Massachusetts.

1969   Incorporates the Mark Rothko Foundation in June. Receives Doctor of Fine Arts honorary degree at Yale University, June 9. Donates nine works originally intended for the Seagram Building to the Tate Gallery, London, stipulating that the paintings always be shown in a room of their own.

1970   Commits suicide February 25. Rothko room at the Tate Gallery opens May 29.

1971   The Rothko Chapel, Houston, Texas, dedicated February 27–28.

1978   Retrospective exhibition at the Solomon R. Guggenheim Museum, New York, October 27–January 14, 1979; later at The Museum of Fine Arts, Houston, Walter Art Center, Minneapolis, and Los Angeles County Museum of Art.

217

INDEX

Fra Angelico, 129, 137, 147, 148, 149, 150, 170, 177, 181, 198
Frazer, W. G., 40, 41
Freud, Sigmund, 20, 54

Gable, Clark, 11
Galerie Bonaparte, 35
Galla Placidia, 71
Gallery Secession, 33
Gauguin, Paul, 114
Genet, Jean, 193, 194
George, Waldemar, 35, 61
German Expressionists, 16, 21, 34
Giacometti, Alberto, 126, 156, 189
Gide, André, 118
Glarner, Fritz, 175
The Golden Bough, 40
Goldman, Emma, 8, 10, 51
Goldwater, Robert, 119, 165, 190
Goodman, Paul, 112
Goodrich, Lloyd, 130
Gorky, Arshile, 97, 99, 102
Gottlieb, Adolph, 23, 25, 33, 34, 39, 65, 67, 73, 75, 76, 77, 78, 80, 81, 82, 90, 93, 96, 98, 101, 102
Goya, Francisco, 75
Graham, John, 32
Greco-Roman art, 59
Greenberg, Clement, 82, 109, 110, 118
Greene, Balcomb, 34, 67
Greek Tragedy, 68
Gregory of Nazianzus, 171
Gregory of Nyssa, 171
Gromaire, Marcel, 69
Gropper, William, 31
Guggenheim, Peggy, 4, 69, 71, 93
Guston, Philip, 118, 130, 131, 167, 174

Haftmann, Werner, 177, 178
Haida Indians, 73
Hamlet, 56, 123
Hare, David, 109
d'Harnancourt, René, 112

Harris, Louis, 16, 25, 33, 67, 68
Hartley, Marsden, 12
Hays, H. R., 31
Hays, Mrs. H. R., 31, 32
Haywood, William, 8, 10
Heidegger, Martin, 186, 191
Hess, Thomas B., 117, 126, 162
"Hierarchical Birds," 83
Hölderlin, Friedrich, 174
Holocaust, 43, 178
Holyoke Center, Harvard, 158
Homer, 59, 93
Hopi, 69
"Horizontal Phantom," 73
House of Mysteries, 115
Houston Chapel, 183, 187
The Hunter (Catalan Landscape), 62, 63
Hunter, Sam, 105
"Hymn to Joy," 54

Impressionism, 11
Indian, American, 18
Industrial Workers of the World, 8
Iphigenia, 44, 75
"The Irrascibles," 133
I.W.W., 9

Jaeger, Werner, 170
James, William, 82
Jazz Age, 21
Jewell, Edward Alden, 75, 76, 78
Johnson, Philip, 146, 169, 183
Jones, Joe, 31
Joyce, James, 40, 41, 175, 176
Jung, Gustav, 54

Kabbalah, 197
Kafka, Franz, 3, 83, 131, 155
Kainen, Jacob, 39
Kandinsky, Wassily, 75
Karfiol, Bernard, 18
Kaufman, Louis, 21
Keats, John, 71